PRAISE FOR
GOD BLESS YOU

God Bless You is wonderfully basic in its presentation of understanding blessings, both natural and spiritual, and how they can affect a life. As a mother and grandmother, I heartily agree with the chapter regarding blessing children. The illustration of the Korean girl who found Christ as her Savior by reading my husband Bill's writing of the Four Spiritual Laws was a blessing to me. Her deep desire to tell my husband thank-you was carried out when Elmer told us this story. It was a small thing, but that is what a blessing can be—a small thing with great results! Read and apply this book to be blessed and to be a blessing.

VONETTE Z. BRIGHT
COFOUNDER, CAMPUS CRUSADE FOR CHRIST
LAKE HART, FLORIDA

GOD BLESS YOU

ELMER L. TOWNS

Regal

From Gospel Light
Ventura, California, U.S.A.

PUBLISHED BY REGAL BOOKS
VENTURA, CALIFORNIA, U.S.A.
PRINTED IN THE U.S.A.

Regal Books is a ministry of Gospel Light, an evangelical Christian publisher dedicated to serving the local church. We believe God's vision for Gospel Light is to provide church leaders with biblical, user-friendly materials that will help them evangelize, disciple and minister to children, youth and families.

It is our prayer that this Regal book will help you discover biblical truth for your own life and help you meet the needs of others. May God richly bless you.

For a free catalog of resources from Regal Books/Gospel Light, please call your Christian supplier or contact us at 1-800-4-GOSPEL or www.regalbooks.com.

Cover and interior design by Robert Williams
Edited by Ron Durham

LIBRARY OF CONGRESS CATALOGING-IN-PUBLICATION DATA
Towns, Elmer L.
    God bless you : how to give and receive blessings / Elmer L. Towns.
        p. cm.
Includes bibliographical references and index.
    ISBN 0-8307-3082-6
    1. Benediction.   I. Title.
    BV199.B4 T68 2003
    248.3—dc21   2002015867

1 2 3 4 5 6 7 8 9 10 11 12 13 14 15 / 09 08 07 06 05 04 03 02

Rights for publishing this book in other languages are contracted by Gospel Light Worldwide, the international nonprofit ministry of Gospel Light. Gospel Light Worldwide also provides publishing and technical assistance to international publishers dedicated to producing Sunday School and Vacation Bible School curricula and books in the languages of the world. For additional information, visit www.gospellightworldwide.org; write to Gospel Light Worldwide, P.O. Box 3875, Ventura, CA 93006; or send an e-mail to info@gospellightworldwide.org.

CONTENTS

Chapter 1 11

What Do You Mean by "God Bless You"?

When you bless others, you are asking God to add value, prosper, protect or develop them spiritually. This book has three assumptions: (1) God will bless people; (2) He uses people to bless others; and (3) you can add value to the lives of others as you bless them.

Chapter 2 22

The Five Laws of Blessing Others

God wants to bless everyone, and He has given principles that we must follow when extending His blessing to them. When we follow God's prescription, we release His prosperity into the lives of others.

Chapter 3 46

How to Add Value to Others

By learning to follow five principles, we can add value, both natural and supernatural, to others.

Chapter 4 68

What Happens When You Bless Others?

When you bless others, you add value to both your life and theirs. That value can take on very practical manifestations.

Chapter 5 89

How to Bless Children

Children are blessed of God, and we as adults can share in blessing them.

Chapter 6 114

You Can Receive the Blessings of Abraham

God gave seven promises to Abraham. You can share in them because "they which be of faith are blessed with faithful Abraham" (Gal. 3:9, KJV).

INTRODUCTION

As I began teaching a series in my Sunday School class on the topic "God Bless You," several in the class responded in the same way: "Gesundheit."

At first I was puzzled by their response. I was talking about divine favor and they were talking about sneezing! Then someone reminded me that responding to someone's sneeze with the German word "gesundheit" actually implies "God bless you." I looked up the origin of "gesundheit" and found that it simply means "health" or "wholesomeness." Before the days of medical technology, a common superstitious belief was that when you sneezed, you blew the soul out of your body; therefore, people would say "God bless you" for spiritual protection—to keep the devil or demons from flying down your throat.

Another belief was that when you sneezed people would think you were near death, and they would say "God bless you" in your moment of crisis so that you would be restored to health.

This Sunday School series on God Bless You was one of the most popular with class members. For the first time, they really understood the weight of saying "God bless you" to someone.

Many people today seem to be more aware of the blessing of God than in the past. At one time, evangelicals reacted against the formal liturgy of high churches and their methods of ceremonial blessing. As a result, many Christians turned their backs on the possibility of blessing others at all. However, the book by Gary Smalley and John Trent, *The Gift of the Blessing*,[1] focused evangelicals' attention upon the need for blessing children in formal ways. That is a book you should read, along with Jack Hayford's book *Blessing Your Children*.[2]

Today, many parents are deeply concerned about their children. They want to protect them from evil in a world of school shootings, drugs, free sex and other temptations. Parents want to make sure their children live Christian lives in a non-Christian world. Mothers have a special concern in this area, and they will find in this book several suggestions for protecting their children with blessings. This book will also be used by fathers in the actual blessing of their children (see "protect-blessing" in the glossary). Because of the large number of single parents today, this book will not be slanted toward either parent.

Formally blessing a child, or anyone else for that matter, should not be thought of as a "rabbit's foot" or other talisman with magical protective powers. Speaking a blessing into the life of a child or anyone else is powerful only by faith in God and *His* power, not the power of any formula. But praying a blessing *in faith* is one way to invoke God's power in protecting our children from evil. It can be a defense against the growing scourge of peer violence, drug abuse, sexual abuse, child abuse, satanism and homosexuality. Blessings spoken in faith can also help children live for God in a godless world that is lawless and bent on evil.

I urge you to study the special blessings in the appendix of this book as well as the definitions of the terms in the glossary. These terms are included to help you understand the various dimensions of blessing others. For example, to "speak-bless" is to say the blessing aloud over the blessee. You "faith-bless" when you know that God has heard your blessing and will do it. You "natural-bless" by doing normal things to add blessing to someone's life. You "spiritual-bless" to help others know God and grow in the Lord. When you "presence-bless" you are speaking God's presence into another's life, and when the recipient "appropriates-bless," he or she acts on the blessing, and both the blessee and the blessor are blessed. To "prosper-bless" is to pray physical blessings on others, and to "protect-bless" is to pray for a spiritual hedge about others to protect them from harm.

This is a short book, and you can read it quickly; but the results of the blessings that this material sets in motion will last a lifetime. Small groups or Bible classes can use it as a study guide and can benefit from topic discussion, while individuals can use it for personal reflection and growth.

I trust you will enjoy reading this book as much as I enjoyed writing it. I hope it changes your life as it has changed mine—by encouraging you to be a positive influence in the lives of others by seeking for them the blessing of God.

Elmer Towns
Written at my home at the foot of
the Blue Ridge Mountains
Summer, 2002

CHAPTER 1

WHAT DO YOU MEAN BY "GOD BLESS YOU"?

What does "God bless you" really mean? When I walk through my Sunday school class before teaching, I say to many people, "God bless you." What do I mean?

When I was a boy growing up, my mother would ask Uncle Herman to bless the food before a meal. We would all bow our heads and he would begin, "Lord, bless this food that we're about to partake, and bless the hands that have made it." What do you mean when you bless food?

BIBLICAL BACKGROUND OF "BLESSING"

The Old Testament word "blessing" comes from a Hebrew word which means "to kneel," as when people would kneel before a king when making a request. Perhaps they were looking for money, a higher position, honor or some other blessing—some "added value" to their life. By kneeling before the king they were in a sense "blessing" him by honoring him. Of course, in return they hoped the king would bless them. It is in this sense that mere humans can be exhorted to "bless the LORD" and "bless His holy name" (Ps. 103:1)—not that we can give God any "added value," but that we kneel before Him in worship.

So the word "blessed" in Scripture includes so much more than what we imply by the marketing phrase "added value" today. God promised to bless His Old Testament people in countless ways and circumstances if they would but follow him:

> Blessed shall you be in the city, and blessed shall you be in the country. Blessed shall be the fruit of your body, the produce of your ground and the increase of your herds, . . . Blessed shall be your basket and your kneading bowl. The LORD will open to you His good treasure, the heavens, to give the rain to your land in its season, and to bless all the work of your hand (Deut. 28:3-5,12).

The whole range of blessings included in this concept is so broad that it comes close to the Hebrew word *shalom*, often translated "peace." However, "peace" is a term much broader and richer than merely not being at war. When God blesses His people—or gives them peace—He grants them a *state of being* that is at rest, secure and wholly protected in Him. So it's natural that the two words "bless" and "peace" often come together, as in Psalm 29:11: "The LORD will bless his people with peace."

In the New Testament, the word "blessing" comes from the Greek word *eulogeo*. This term consists of the prefix *eu*, which means "good," and *logeo*, "to speak." So when you bless someone, you "speak goodness" into his or her life.

THE IMPORTANCE OF WORDS

This reminds us of the importance the Bible places on the act of speaking itself—the very use of words. Jesus said:

> But I say to you that for every idle word men may speak, they will give account of it in the day of judgment. For by your words you will be justified, and by your words you will be condemned (Matt. 12:36-37).

Jesus vested special power in the words of His apostles. After Peter had made the good confession (see Matt. 16:13-20), Jesus promised that "whatever you bind on earth will be bound in heaven, and whatever you loose on earth will be loosed in heaven" (Matt. 16:19).

The Bible concept of the power of words is rooted in the power of the Word of God, by which the worlds were spoken into existence. Of course, as humans, we don't quite have that power! However, our words are a reflection of the power of *the* Word. Whether we use our tongues to bless or to curse, something of the creative power of God clings to our human speech. Speaking is serious business! Speaking is often the way God makes pronouncements upon us, and there are echoes of His voice of judgment or grace when we speak words over others.

That old saying from our childhood, Sticks and stones may break my bones, but words can never hurt me, is simply false! I hope that one result of this book is that you become more sensitive to the power of your own words to hurt or heal.

The grandest example of the power to bless is the gift of God's Son as He blesses us or speaks good into our lives in the gift of salvation: "God, having raised up His Servant Jesus, sent Him to bless you, in turning away every one of you from your iniquities" (Acts 3:26).

So when I say to the people in my Sunday school class, "God bless you," I have in mind both the added value of external blessings and something much more rich and full. I do want God to prosper them, and perhaps to give them physical health, or to bless their relationships with others. But in a fuller sense I am "kneeling" before God to ask Him to "speak good" in the lives of these people I love—give more of *Himself* to them—to bless them in the sense of surrounding them with His presence, mercy, grace and peace and to fill their lives with all good things.

> Saying "God bless you" is
> one person speaking good words into
> the life of another.

One of the most familiar pictures of Jesus from the New Testament is His blessing children. "[Jesus] took [the children] up in His arms, laid His hands on them, and blessed them" (Mark 10:16). Notice what Jesus did. He was one person speaking good words into the lives of children. What did He do when He blessed them? He was causing them to be happy, to prosper. He was giving of Himself to add value to their lives.

DIMENSIONS OF BLESSINGS

There is nothing miraculous about blessing others. A blessing is not a miracle. However, just as ice and water come from the same origin but are different in feel and substance, so a blessing and a miracle are similar. Ice is made up of water, but it is in a different form; likewise a miracle is a blessing from God, but more intense in feel and substance.

The Differences

- A blessing is good, but a miraculous intervention is much more.
- A blessing is God's prosperity, but a supernatural deliverance from trouble is much more.
- The blessing of a fellow believer ministers added value, but when God solves a problem, it is much more.
- A blessing invokes God's increase, but deliverance from addiction is much more.

These facts about what a blessing is *not* tell us that there is much more to Christianity than blessing others. However, when God supernaturally intervenes or delivers you from trouble, one of the outcomes of course is that you are blessed by God. All supernatural works of God are a blessing to the recipient. But when God's people pronounce a blessing on someone, it's a much milder work. A blessing is simply one person calling on a sovereign God to add value to another's life.

On a hot, sultry day a golfer suffers heatstroke that leads to a heart attack. He doesn't just need a blessing; he needs a prayer of healing. He needs an ambulance. Another golfer finds his way to the shade of a large tree on a hill where he enjoys a cool breeze.

The temperature is reduced from 90 degrees to 80 degrees; that's a blessing. The breeze adds value to his life.

A man who is starving to death doesn't just need a blessing; he needs food. And when something to eat is given to him, he gobbles it down, not thinking of its taste. The food saves his life.

In another setting, I may eat a bowl of cereal and milk late at night before I go to bed. The food doesn't save my life, nor is it a miraculous intervention. My wife cuts a few strawberries into my cereal; that's a blessing. A blessing is added value.

A blessing can consist of natural or spiritual added value. Natural added value influences your everyday life, while spiritual added value influences your relationship to God. Because life is so involved, these two factors often overlap each other.

About 25 years ago I began a practice of naturally blessing my wife early each morning. When I wake—usually five minutes to six—I pray the Lord's Prayer before I get out of bed. After I fill the coffeepot and turn it on, I go get the morning paper and have coffee as I read the paper. Before I go to my study to meet God in my quiet time, I fix another cup of coffee—one teaspoon of cream—and take it to my wife in bed. I want to bless her life and begin her day in an enjoyable way. That's natural added value to her life.

When I meet God in my study, I worship, pray and learn from the Word of God. I am blessed there, too—with spiritual added value.

When you sing "Make me a blessing to someone today" are you wanting to make the life of someone happier, easier or prosperous? That's adding natural value because you are making life easier for him or her. But if you have in mind a spiritual blessing, you are singing about wanting that person to be saved or to grow in Christ.

What is a spiritual blessing? The greatest blessing to anyone is the presence of God in his or her life. We attend many worship services where little seems to happen. Then once in a while you sense God's presence in a special way. You worship freely and spiritually. God pours His Spirit into your life (see Acts 2:17). Some call this experience a revival, but for our purposes we will call it the atmospheric presence of God. Like a cool mist on a hot day, you sometimes experience God's presence in a refreshing way.

You are also seeking to refresh others when you spiritually bless them, speaking Jesus' name over them and in them. You want them to experience God's revitalizing presence. And what does His presence do for them? It guides them, illuminates their spiritual understanding, gives them joy and protects them from the evil one. That's God blessing someone with His presence (see "presence-bless" in the glossary).

The Bible says that God has "blessed us with every spiritual blessing in the heavenly places in Christ" (Eph. 1:3). Notice that you get this blessing *in Christ*. As you hide your life in Christ, He indwells you—"You in Me, and I in you" (John 14:20).

When you say that a sermon was a blessing, what do you mean? Was the message enjoyable, or did you learn something? Maybe God was telling you how to live, how to be a better Christian or how to serve the Lord. That sermon added spiritual value to your life. And what better blessing can you have than God's presence in your life?

Many people bless others by the act of praying for them or by other Christian exercises such as fasting, worship, etc. (see "pray-bless" in the glossary). However, the Bible teaches that there is a definite formal act of blessing another person. It is necessary that we become *intentional* in the formal act of blessing others (see "speak-blessing" in the glossary).

When you bless others, you are speaking God's blessings to them, over them and in them, whether in the form of natural or spiritual added value. You are calling for a special measure of the presence of God in their lives.

TAKE-AWAY VALUES

- God can use your spoken blessing on others to give them a special measure of His covenant-love and to add value to their lives.
- As important as your nonmiraculous blessings are, God can add His mightier miraculous work according to His will.
- You can invoke both natural and spiritual blessings on others.
- To be "in Christ" is to be in the place where you can experience *all* spiritual blessings (see Eph. 1:3).

THREE-STEP BIBLE STUDY

A. *Read* each Bible passage.

B. Use the *question* that follows each passage to analyze the passage.

C. Write your *answer* in the space provided.

1. Deuteronomy 28:3-6,12

> Blessed shall you be in the city, and blessed shall you be in the country. Blessed shall be the fruit of your body, the produce of your ground and the increase of your herds, the increase of your cattle and the offspring of your flocks. Blessed shall be your basket and your kneading bowl. Blessed shall you be when you come in, and blessed shall you be when you go out. The LORD will open to you His good treasure, the heavens, to give the rain to your land in its season, and to bless all the work of your hand.

In what ways did God promise to bless His people?

1.

2.

3.

4.

2. Psalm 103:1-2

> Bless the LORD, O my soul;
> And all that is within me, bless His holy name!
> Bless the LORD, O my soul,
> And forget not all His benefits.

How can a mere human being bless God? (Hint: See page 1 and the meaning of the Hebrew word for "bless.")

3. Matthew 12:36-37

> But I say to you that for every idle word men may speak, they will give account of it in the day of judgment. For by your words you will be justified, and by your words you will be condemned.

How does Jesus emphasize the importance of what we say?

4. Mark 10:16

> And He took [the young children] up in His arms, laid His hands on them, and blessed them.

What added value, or other benefit, do you think this act had on the children and their parents?

5. Ephesians 1:3

Blessed be the God and Father of our Lord Jesus Christ, who has blessed us with every spiritual blessing in the heavenly places in Christ.

What blessings bring added value to our lives if we are "in Christ"?

1.

2.

3.

4.

JOURNALING

Keeping a journal will bless you as you work through this book on blessing. Writing down your thoughts in a separate notebook will clarify them. Use the following questions to guide your thoughts and writings.

1. Do you really believe God wants to bless others, and do you believe God will use you to bless others?
2. When people prosper, do you think they are lucky or do you think God has blessed them?
3. Are the good things that have happened to you the blessing of God?
4. Reflect on the usual tone and pattern of your everyday speech as you interact with others. What improvements can you make by recalling Jesus' words in Matthew 12:36-37 about the importance of our language?

CHAPTER 2

THE FIVE LAWS OF BLESSING OTHERS

"Let me read from your Bible," a pastor said to a bedridden elderly man who had been confined to his home for over three years. Taking the Bible, the pastor turned to a psalm and read from God's Word. At the end of the passage, the pastor remarked, "Start reading at this psalm and I'll be back next month." When the pastor closed the Bible, the old man's feeble hands reached eagerly for the Bible to clench it to his chest.

"Thank you . . . thank you very much." The elderly man grinned like a child with a secret, and he squeezed the Bible to his chest until the pastor left. Then, even before the door was shut behind the pastor, the elderly man's bony fingers feverishly turned to the psalm just read by the pastor. It was there.

A $20 bill.

A few years earlier the pastor had begun to leave money in the Bible after he read a passage while visiting the elderly man, as a way to bless the man who had been faithful in the church for many years. Every time the pastor returned, he would check the passage where he had left the bill. Sure enough, the money was gone.

The elderly man had used the money for special things he liked—a fresh, hot hamburger from his favorite corner grill or doughnuts. The pastor got great satisfaction knowing that the money brought happiness in little ways to a faithful saint.

The money was an example of a natural blessing. When the pastor shared God's promises from the Bible, that was a spiritual blessing.

How did the pastor know what was happening? People have a way of sharing little bits of information like that with their pastor. So, the pastor and his wife watched from their car a few houses away to see what would happen. A grandson had been phoned immediately after the pastor left. The young grandson came to get the money and then rode his bicycle to the corner grill to buy something for Gramps.

I teach the pastor's Sunday School class that meets in the auditorium of our church. Since we are a large church with multiple pastors, some of the class members come to me for pastoral help. I've dedicated several new businesses over the past 17 years. These were secular businesses owned or operated by Christians. When a member's business has a grand opening, I've been invited to bless the new enterprise. After all, if you were investing tens of thousands of dollars in buildings and inventory, wouldn't you want God's blessing on your business (see "agree-bless" in the glossary)?

When my favorite Krispy Kreme doughnut shop opened in Lynchburg, I was asked to bless the business. Often I talk in my Sunday School class about how much I love Krispy Kreme doughnuts, so it was natural to invite me to the grand opening. Instead of a ribbon cutting, a long doughnut chain of actual

Krispy Kreme doughnuts was draped across the front door. I prayed for God to bless and prosper the business, and then the mayor and I cut the doughnut chain with gigantic scissors.

When I blessed an auto-repair shop, I asked God to bless the business, even though money was being made off the misfortune of those who had accidents. I prayed for the owner to help restore lives by evangelism as he restored cars.

My favorite blessing was at the opening of a new bridal shop. A woman in my Sunday School class inherited several thousand dollars when her mother died. She told me of a lifelong dream of owning her own bridal shop and asked if I would bless her business on opening day. I agreed. I prayed for God to bless the new owner as she blessed new marriages, both through her counsel and her sales. Then I prayed for God to bless her financially in the business. She started out the 12th smallest wedding retail shop in Lynchburg, Virginia, with everything she had financially on the line. A decade later she sold it to retire—after it had become the largest bridal shop in the city and her investment had multiplied many times.

God can bless businesses. Those who enter business should plan to follow biblical business principles and ask God to bless the company (see "dedication-bless" in the glossary).

FIVE LAWS ABOUT GOD'S BLESSINGS

- Law 1: God wants to bless people.
- Law 2: God uses His people to bless others.
- Law 3: God's people must be blessed before they can bless others.
- Law 4: To bless others we must follow God's pattern.
- Law 5: Those who are blessed experience improved lives.

Remember: When you bless others, you are not only asking God to make them prosper or calling for added value to their life; but also you are calling for God's presence in, over and through their lives. Therefore, when you naturally bless them, you may be making them happy or making their life easier.

When you do things for others in God's name you spiritually bless them, just as you are blessed when you praise God, read His Word or listen to a sermon. So pray daily, *Lord, help me to add value to the lives of other people.*

LAW 1: GOD WANTS TO BLESS PEOPLE

Some people picture God as a miser sitting in heaven who selfishly hoards all His money. They think He makes up rules just to make people miserable. Those people do not know the God of the Bible. God loves all people and wants to give added value to them as well as to bless them with His presence. If we think of a blessing as money, God wants to share His wealth with everyone. Notice the following pictures:

Physical Blessings
God has promised His people that if you "bring all the tithes into the storehouse, . . . and try Me . . . if I will not open for you the windows of heaven and pour out for you such blessing" (Mal. 3:10).

This is too often twisted by selfishness. Too many people treat the tithe like a lottery ticket, thinking if they give money to God, they might get lucky and get money back. That's not what the verse says. It says that when we tithe, God will give us blessings. That is, He gives added value to our lives in many ways, not just financially. God's blessing may come in the form of money, but it also may be in other things that give us happiness, even as we suffer from a lack of money.

There are missionaries deep in the jungle with few luxuries in life who are some of the happiest people in the world. With no air conditioning, grocery stores, malls or paved roads, they must toil with their hands—repairing their autos without proper tools, washing their clothes without a washer and living without ice cream, doughnuts or all the luxuries we have in America. They still tithe, or give money to God, but they don't get physical things in return. Their greatest joy may be in transforming a spoken language into a written language. They experience greater spiritual blessings when they hear a native read aloud from the Word of God translated into their language than they would if they had material comforts. Surely, the windows of heaven are opened upon those missionaries as God pours out His blessings on them.

Yet God may also bless Americans living in financial prosperity. Think of spending money to show your kids a good time at a theme park, to buy hot dogs or to go to the beach. You spend money on your kids, and they thrill you with their squeals of delight.

In a similar picture, you give God a tithe and He adds value to your life and to the lives of your children. Sometimes the added value is money in return. Sometimes the value is inner contentment and peace "that My joy may remain in you, and that your joy may be full" (John 15:11). Or the blessing may come in the form of seeing your children follow the Lord.

Initially, God was pleased with His creation and He blessed Adam and Eve. "God blessed them; and God said to them, 'Be fruitful and multiply, and fill the earth'" (Gen. 1:28, *NASB*). While this fruitfulness includes having children, it can also be applied to every aspect of replenishing the earth, i.e., taking care of the earth, or of our own garden, so that it will be fruitful and bless others with good food.

Sometimes the blessing of God is good health, as when God protects us from germs and bacteria. Sometimes the blessing of God is physical strength, as God supplies food or uses whatever food we have so that we are strengthened more than might be expected. At other times, the blessing of God is physical stamina so that we have a great desire to serve God, or energy to do the right thing.

Sometimes, of course, we don't feel that we are physically blessed. This doesn't always mean that God has determined not to bless us. As Jesus reminded us, God "sends rain on both the just and on the unjust" (Matt. 5:45). Yet we also must remember that there *may* be a relationship between following God's will and being physically blessed, as we noted from Deuteronomy 28:1-14, regarding physical and spiritual well-being.

The Blessing of Long Life. God has made a general promise that those who obey their parents will live a long time: "Honor your father and your mother, that your days may be long upon the land" (Exod. 20:12). This is not an absolute promise in the sense that those who dishonor their parents will automatically die young while those who honor their parents will surely live many years. But in the Old Testament there does seem to be a link between obedience and a long life. People who obey their parents generally have a good, peaceful life that leads to physical longevity. Notice the following blessing:

> The Lord bless you out of Zion,
> And may you see the good of Jerusalem
> All the days of your life.
> Yes, may you see your children's children (Ps. 128:5-6).

The Blessing of a Happy Countenance. Our internal experience is reflected in our outer appearance. When we are discouraged, it shows in our face and in our actions—even our physical bodies lack energy. But when we hear good news, suddenly we're "pumped" and motivated, and we want to dance on the air.

"A merry heart makes a cheerful countenance" (Prov. 15:13).

Therefore, your face mirrors the blessings of God. When you are blessed spiritually, it shows and you look happy—your fears are gone, your stress is relieved and your burdens are lifted. So rejoice, because God has "blessed us with every spiritual blessing" (Eph. 1:3).

Spiritual Blessings

As we noted in chapter 1, God "has blessed us with every spiritual blessing in the heavenly places in Christ" (Eph. 1:3). Christians are heirs to God's great blessing-promise to Abraham: "In you all the families of the earth shall be blessed" (Gen. 12:3; see Gal. 3:6-9). Although we may rightly think of salvation as being the chief of these blessings, think of the many other ways God blesses us spiritually.

God blesses those who follow His principles of human relationships with happy homes and happy church fellowships—*blessed* relationships. Isn't this a wonderful blessing?

God gives courage, a spiritual blessing to the fainthearted, "So we may boldly say; 'The LORD is my helper; I will not fear. What can man do to me?'" (Heb. 13:6, see Ps. 118:6). And again, "God has not given us a spirit of fear, but of power and of love and of a sound mind" (2 Tim. 1:7).

God gives us the unsurpassed spiritual blessings of faith, hope and love. I often think of the blessing of hope in times when a faithful loved one dies. At such times, it is a blessing of infinite added value that we do not "sorrow as others who have no hope" (1 Thess. 4:13).

The Blessing of Influence. God can bless you by using your influence in the lives of others. God promised Abraham, "I will make you a great nation; I will bless you and make your name great" (Gen. 12:2). Just as Abraham became one of the best-known names in

Judaism, Islam and Christianity and influenced those religions, God can bless and use your influence in the lives of others.

LAW 2: GOD USES HIS PEOPLE TO BLESS OTHERS

Anyone can be a blessing to others. No matter who you are; you can be a blessing to others. No matter how young, how immature in the faith, how elderly, how busy, how skilled or how unskilled, you can bless others.

You Can Bless Your Friends

In Genesis 14, the Bible says that Melchizedek, king of Salem (which would become Jerusalem), blessed Abraham (when he was still called Abram). Abraham had just returned from winning a great battle over five nations from Mesopotamia. As ruler of a nomadic tribe, Abraham rescued his nephew Lot from the clutches of his enemies in an area ruled by Melchizedek. Returning from battle, he gave a tenth of the spoils—a king's share—to Melchizedek, over the king's protest. And the king, though not a part of Israel, blessed Abraham.

First, the king gave Abraham a natural blessing, providing him with a meal of bread and wine. Then Melchizedek blessed both Abraham and Abraham's God, saying:

Blessed be Abram of God Most High,
Possessor of heaven and earth;
And blessed be God Most High,
Who has delivered your enemies into your hand (Gen. 14:19-20).

Just as Abraham and Melchizedek were friends—yet blessed each other, you can bless your friends by helping them during difficulties and looking after their material possessions (as did Abraham), or providing a meal and expressing prayers for your friend (as did Melchizedek).

Fathers Can Bless Their Children

The book of Genesis contains several stories of fathers blessing their sons. One of those is mentioned in the New Testament also, for we are told that "by faith Isaac blessed Jacob" (Heb. 11:20). Isaac prayed that Jacob would inherit his own legacy, connected as it was to God's promises.

On this basis, shouldn't a father bless his children today? Yes! A father should add value to his children naturally by endowing them with physical and material things. A father should also add value spiritually to his children by training, teaching and praying for them, and by being obedient to the Lord.

Grandfathers Can Bless their Grandchildren

The Bible contains the story of grandfather Jacob blessing his two grandsons: "By faith Jacob . . . blessed each of the sons of Joseph" (Heb. 11:21). Shouldn't a grandfather be concerned about his grandchildren, both naturally and spiritually? Yes! A grandfather should add value to his grandchildren in many ways. Perhaps he can leave them an inheritance, just as God does His own children, "that I may cause those who love me to inherit wealth, that I may fill their treasuries" (Prov. 8:21).

Christian Leaders Can Bless Worshipers

Old Testament priests were commanded, "You shall bless the children of Israel" (Num. 6:23), saying:

> The LORD bless you and keep you;
> The LORD make His face shine upon you,
> And be gracious to you;

The LORD lift up His countenance upon you,
And give you peace (Num. 6:24-26).

I was a young 19-year-old preacher during my second year in college, pastoring the Westminster Presbyterian Church in Savannah, Georgia. Quite often I would repeat this Levitical benediction at the end of worship services. I really didn't understand the significance of it, but I have come to realize

> **I can speak the Lord's presence into people's lives if my spirit is willing.**

that I can speak the Lord's presence into people's lives if my spirit is willing. And if the people will receive it, God will do something for them in the coming week they would not have experienced without the blessing. God would often add both natural and spiritual prosperity to them (see "benediction-bless" in the glossary).

Jesus Blessed People

When the disciples were frustrated with the children surrounding Jesus, they tried to break up the crowd. But Jesus stopped them. He said, "Let the little children come to Me, and do not forbid them; for of such is the kingdom of God" (Mark 10:14). Then out of love for the children and what He could do for them, "He took them up in His arms, laid His hands on them, and blessed them" (Mark 10:16).

The very last act of Jesus on Earth was to bless His disciples. Right before He ascended up into Heaven, "He led them out as far as Bethany, and He lifted up His hands and blessed them. Now it came to pass, while He blessed them, that He was parted from them and carried up into heaven" (Luke 24:50-51).

LAW 3: GOD'S PEOPLE MUST BE BLESSED BEFORE THEY CAN BLESS OTHERS

You can't give to others what you haven't experienced. Just as you must play golf before you can teach it, and you must be able to drive a car before you give your children driving lessons, you must experience God's blessings before you bless others.

Jacob was a rebellious kid growing up in a family where the evident blessing of God was on his grandfather Abraham and his father, Isaac. But Jacob ran away from his family and worked for his uncle Laban for seven years to earn a dowry for his anticipated wife, Rachel. Most people know how Jacob's uncle Laban tricked the trickster Jacob by substituting Rachel's older sister Leah in the marriage tent. Young Jacob had to work another seven years for Rachel.

Then as Jacob continued to work for his uncle Laban, the Lord blessed and prospered Laban's activity because of Jacob. Laban testified, "I have learned by experience that the LORD has blessed me for your sake" (Gen. 30:27). What does that mean? God had promised to bless Jacob (see Gen. 28:3), and He did. Then as Jacob, who was blessed of God, worked for his uncle Laban, the blessing "spilled over" onto Laban, and he received a financial blessing.

Have you been blessed of God? If so, now you must bless others. You must pass it on. What you get from God you are to pass on to other people. You pass on your own blessings in the way of learned lessons, accumulated wisdom and meaningful experiences. The apostle Paul taught the young minister Timothy this: "And the things that you have heard from me among many witnesses, commit these to faithful men who will be able to teach others also" (2 Tim. 2:2).

Selfish people can't give. They are like a vacuum, drawing everything into their own web of experiences. They are like the black holes in space, sucking everything near them into their center. Black holes have tremendous heat, because everything that is sucked in is immediately burned up. Eventually a black hole implodes upon itself. Is that not like selfish people? Do they not eventually implode upon themselves because their selfish glory gives them little satisfaction when it is obtained by fleshly means?

The more blessings you give to others, the stronger internally you become yourself. So learn to bless others, and in the process you will bless yourself by adding value to your life—but only after you have added value to the lives of others.

LAW 4: TO BLESS OTHERS WE MUST FOLLOW GOD'S PATTERN

Just because you say "God bless you" doesn't mean that God will act on that saying. Just as you must pray in Jesus' name to get answers to your prayers, so you must learn to bless following God's formula. Then you will add value to other people. Failing to bless others according to God's will results in no blessing at all. For example, there are many shallow actions that don't bless others at all:

- Making the sign of a cross in a superstitious way.
- Having people touch or hold the Bible as a fetish.
- Saying empty words, such as "blessings on you," when you don't live their meaning.

Use God's Name to Bless

When you bless another, make sure you do it in Jesus' name. Obviously, you do not bless others out of your own ability or "superior" spirituality. God told the priest, "So they shall put My name on the children of Israel, and *I* will bless them" (Num. 6:27, emphasis added). So when you say "God bless you," make sure that you are pointing people to Jesus and not relying on your own ability (see "intercede-bless" in the glossary).

Speak Blessing in Faith

When you are blessing someone, you must trust God to fulfill your spoken blessing. Notice Isaac's story: "By faith Isaac blessed Jacob . . . concerning things to come" (Heb. 11:20). Isaac had enough faith to believe that God would bless his son with the promise given to his grandfather Abraham. Jacob also believed in God's integrity that He would bless his sons as well. The patriarchs could bless their sons concerning things to come because they believed that God controlled the future (see "faith-bless" in the glossary).

Since *receiving* a blessing is tied to faith, we should not be surprised that *giving* a blessing is, too. Notice the conditions of the blessing promised in God's covenant:

> Now it shall come to pass, if you diligently obey the voice of the LORD your God, to observe carefully all His commandments which I command you today, that the LORD your God will set you high above all nations of the earth. And all these blessings shall come upon you and overtake you, because you obey the voice of the LORD your God (Deut. 28:1-2).

Receiving a blessing is tied to heartfelt obedience to God, which is the first step of faith (see "appropriate-bless" in the glossary). The same condition is tied to your spoken faith. "If you have faith as a mustard seed, you will say to this mountain, 'Move from here to there,' and it will move; and nothing will be impossible for you" (Matt. 17:20). Notice the conditions are that you must have faith and that you must speak what you want done. Then God will do what you ask in faith. Therefore, when you bless others, you must first have faith in God; then you must speak the blessing into their lives and expect God to fulfill it. When you do that, God will fulfill your request by carrying out the blessing.

Use the Bible in Blessing

When you speak God's Word into people's lives, make sure they not only hear the Bible, but also understand how to apply it to their lives. The book of Revelation gives the promise, "Blessed is he who reads and those who hear the words of this prophecy, and keep those things which are written in it" (Rev. 1:3). A person must either read the Bible or listen to it being read and obey the things written in the Scriptures to receive a blessing from Scripture. Since "the Word of God is alive and powerful" (Heb. 4:12, author's translation), then speak God's Word into others' lives to produce the changes it promises.

Also, remember that the Word of God equips you to be prepared against the devil's schemes. The psalmist said, "Your word I have hidden in my heart, that I might not sin against You" (Ps. 119:11). Therefore, when you bless people with the Word of God, you can also pray for God to keep them from the evil one.[1]

Speak Prayers Out Loud in Blessing

The blessing of God is not automatic. You receive it by faith from God when you ask for it. When Jesus fed the multitude with five loaves and two fishes, "He looked up to heaven, blessed and broke the loaves" (Mark 6:41). Even Jesus had to speak a prayer when He wanted to bless.

Prayer means many things: intimacy with God, worshiping God, intercession and getting things from God. Because of all of these, when you pray, you are being blessed by God. And in praying aloud, you are able to bless others. When you speak a prayer of blessing upon others, you are getting things from God to pass on to them.

Of course the blessing does not come through you as a conduit but descends directly from God upon the person. Every person has immediate and direct access to God. You are not the mediator, nor is any other person who speaks a blessing. There is "one God and one Mediator between God and men, the Man Christ Jesus" (1 Tim. 2:5).

This does not mean you will never be used by God. For example, God may call you to give others needed money, and in doing so, He blesses them. You can be used of God to bless a person, but the blessing comes from God. He is the blessor, the recipient is the blessee. You are the servant of God.

LAW 5: THOSE WHO ARE BLESSED EXPERIENCE IMPROVED LIVES

God's Blessing Often Brings Prosperity
Notice what God did in the case of Potiphar: "The LORD blessed the Egyptian's house for Joseph's sake; and the blessing of the LORD was on all that he had in the house and in the field" (Gen. 39:5). The blessing of God on Joseph's life overflowed to a general blessing on all Potiphar had.

However, some are blessed apart from financial prosperity. The thief who is serving time in prison becomes born-again. His life is turned around, and he becomes honest and trustworthy because of Jesus Christ. He is then blessed with the position of trustee. He wasn't blessed with financial rewards, but he was blessed with a greater degree of freedom and responsibility. If the parole board gives him an early release, it's a blessing tied to salvation and growth in character.

A material blessing on a business leader is mentioned in the book of Ruth. Boaz was a man who had God's blessing upon his life, and he was also "a man of great wealth" (Ruth 2:1). Notice the fruit of God's blessing in the life of Boaz: "And [his workers] answered him, 'The LORD bless you!'" (Ruth 2:4).

Since God can bless business owners, or employers, perhaps you ought to pray for your employer. Ask God to add value to your employer, and when your employer prospers in his business, you will prosper.

God also blesses workers: "Blessed shall you be in the country" (Deut. 28:3). This means that those who work can have the added value of God's presence in their lives. When they become more productive, they add to the bottom line of profits, and therefore, they add to the capital worth of the company. So, if you are a boss, or employer, speak God's blessings into the lives of your workers. In the end, your business will be blessed.

Job had the blessing of God upon his labor. Judging from the Scriptures, he first worked with his hands: "[The Lord has] blessed the work of [Job's] hands" (Job 1:10). Job eventually became wealthy working with his hands. Why did God bless Job? "[Job] was perfect and upright, and one who feared God, and hated evil" (Job 1:1, author's translation). God blessed Job because of his character and spirituality.

Notice what else the blessing of God did for Job: "Have You not made a hedge around him, around his household, and around all that he has on every side?" (Job 1:10; see "protect-bless" in the glossary). God protected Job's increase in wealth while He prospered Job's ability to gain wealth.

God Blesses through Children

God has promised to bless us through the children that He gives to us (see appendix). Our children bring us joy, make us grow spiritually and stretch us in every way of life. We get contentment as we see our children and our children's children serve the Lord.

> Behold, children are a heritage from the LORD,
> The fruit of the womb is a reward.
> Like arrows in the hand of a warrior,
> So are the children of one's youth.
> Happy is the man who has his quiver full of them;
> They shall not be ashamed,
> But shall speak with their enemies in the gate (Ps. 127:3-5).

The Financial Blessing of God:
God helped Job gain wealth; God protected
Job's attained wealth.

THE TESTIMONY OF EXPERIENCE

I know that God has richly blessed my life because I've experienced it. I believe I have good health, I have been able to make what money that has come to me go a long way, I've had success in the Lord's work and I've been blessed with three wonderful children. However, some might scoff at what I consider blessings and label them accidental. My health, they might say, is the result of good genes. They might say I was taught how to manage my money properly or that I've been successful in my ministry because I've disciplined my time. They may look at all I do and say it is the result of hard work. There are skeptics who do not believe God adds value to life. They will not accept the things we say about the blessing of God.

So, what is your response to these scoffers? First of all, you don't have to respond. You don't need to answer them. Since you serve the Lord, you answer only to Him. Look in your heart and ask yourself, *Have I been blessed of God, and do I know it?* Only you can answer that question. I've answered the question, *yes!* I know God has blessed me.

Second, you can pray for the scoffers, that God would open their eyes to give them understanding. "Bless those who curse you, and pray for those who spitefully use you" (Luke 6:28). Not only can you pray that they understand the blessing of God, but also you can pray that they be convicted of their sin and have a desire for God's best in their lives.

Third, when scoffers question you and you don't have an answer, refuse to let them discourage you. Continue to live by faith, serve the Lord in integrity and obey the Word of God. There is nothing else you can do but to keep your eyes on the Lord and serve Him faithfully.

TAKE-AWAY VALUES

- I can be used of God to bless others.
- God wants to use me to bless others.
- I must receive blessings from God before I give them.
- I can receive spiritual and natural blessings.
- I must follow God's formula to bless others.
- I improve the lives of others by blessing them.

THREE-STEP BIBLE STUDY

A. *Read* each Bible passage.

B. Use the *question* that follows each passage to analyze the passage.

C. Write your *answer* in the space provided.

1. Genesis 1:28-29

> Then God blessed them, and God said to them, "Be fruitful and multiply; fill the earth and subdue it; have dominion over the fish of the sea, over the birds of the air, and over every living thing that moves on the earth." And God said, "See, I have given you every herb that yields seed which is on the face of all the earth, and every tree whose fruit yields seed; to you it shall be for food."

How did God bless Adam and Eve?

2. Psalm 128:5-6

> The LORD bless you out of Zion,
> And may you see the good of Jerusalem
> All the days of your life.
> Yes, may you see your children's children.
> Peace be upon Israel!

What aspects of your family are included in God's blessing?

3. Hebrews 11:20-21

> By faith Isaac blessed Jacob and Esau concerning things to come. By faith Jacob, when he was dying, blessed each of the sons of Joseph, and worshiped, leaning on the top of his staff.

What can you learn from the lives of the patriarchs that is an example of parents blessing their children?

4. Numbers 6:24-26

> The LORD bless you and keep you;
> The LORD make His face shine upon you,
> And be gracious to you;
> The LORD lift up His countenance upon you,
> And give you peace.

What blessing is suggested here that you can give to someone?

5. Mark 10:14,16

> But when Jesus saw it, He was greatly displeased and said to them, "Let the little children come to Me, and do not forbid them; for of such is the kingdom of God." And He took them up in His arms, laid His hands on them, and blessed them.

Why would Jesus bless children, and how can we do so today?

6. Genesis 30:27 and 39:5

> And Laban said to him, "Please stay, if I have found favor in your eyes, for I have learned by experience that the LORD has blessed me for your sake." So it was, from the time that he had made him overseer of his house and all that he had, that the LORD blessed the Egyptian's house for Joseph's sake; and the blessing of the LORD was on all that he had in the house and in the field.

God blessed the employer of both Jacob and Joseph. What does that mean for your job and the place where you work?

7. Numbers 6:27

> So they shall put My name on the children of Israel, and I will bless them.

How can you speak the name of God on those you bless?

JOURNALING

Use the following questions to guide your thoughts and writings in your separate journal.

1. Write down some ways God has used you to bless others this week. Were they mostly natural blessings or spiritual blessings?

2. How has God blessed your life this week? In what ways did He bless you naturally? Spiritually?

3. Who did God use to bless your life this week? How did God use them? What do you feel about the person who blessed you? How have you grown in recognizing these people?

4. How do you feel about speaking aloud your blessing on someone else (e.g., embarrassed; unworthy; hesitant; confident; other)?

5. How can you adjust your life to put yourself in a better position to bless others by becoming more obedient to God's will?

6. How do you react when you hear someone credit "luck" or "being worthy" in situations where you believe God has actually been actively blessing them? How can you use the suggestions at the end of this chapter to adjust this reaction?

HOW TO ADD VALUE TO OTHERS

My wife, Ruth, loves to bless our daughter, Debbie J. Once a week my wife, Ruth, goes out to help Debbie clean out the great big old house in the country where Debbie lives. Maybe Debbie wouldn't do it without her mother, or maybe it's a blessing to Debbie just to be with her mother. It may even be that Debbie is a better wife because the old rooms are being refurbished.

Just as Ruth helps Debbie, you can bless someone naturally when you help him or her accomplish in life what he or she wants to accomplish.

Both my son, Sam, and his wife work outside the home, and they need someone to pick up their children from child care and watch them until one or the other gets home. My wife, Ruth, loves to pick up her grandchildren, and sometimes we meet for dinner at the local hamburger place. My son says that Ruth is a natural blessing because she makes life easier for his family. But more than a baby-sitter, Ruth gives her love and grandmotherly spiritual wisdom to her two grandchildren. This is a spiritual blessing.

Ruth's hairdresser is a single mom. With most customers she just chats about a variety of things. But when Ruth sits in the chair, the hairdresser pours out her heart to Ruth concerning problems and challenges. The hairdresser says that Ruth is a natural blessing to her just because she listens. When Ruth gives biblical answers, she is also a spiritual blessing. And because of these natural blessings and spiritual blessings, when Ruth leaves, the hairdresser is happier, has gained understanding and is better able to cope with the stress in her life.

When you bless others, you add value to their life, or in a biblical sense, you prosper them naturally or spiritually. Most of us go through life trying to be happy or to get ahead; but we become more successful in our Christian life when we make everything and everyone around us a little bit better—when we try to be a blessing to them.

There's an old hymn called "Make Me a Blessing to Someone Today." This means we want to help people improve their lives, to make life easier, to make them happier or to bring them a spiritual blessing. How can we do that?

FIVE PRINCIPLES FOR ADDING VALUE TO OTHERS

- Principle 1: You begin to bless others when you value them.
- Principle 2: You bless others when you initiate faith in them.
- Principle 3: You bless others by making yourself valuable to them.

- Principle 4: You bless others when you know and relate to their needs and desires.
- Principle 5: You bless others when you help them fulfill God's purpose in their lives.

PRINCIPLE 1: YOU BEGIN TO BLESS OTHERS WHEN YOU VALUE THEM

Remember that the essence of Christianity is *relationships*. Some people reject that statement, insisting that Christianity is orthodox doctrine, or that its essence is the historic event of the death of Jesus Christ on the cross. Certainly doctrine and the Cross are objectively a part of the faith. True Christianity consists of sound biblical doctrine that keeps the sacrificial death of Christ for us at the center.

But sound doctrine and faith in the objective event of the Cross do not reach other persons without relationships. When someone influenced you to become a Christian, or actually led you to Christ, that person formed a relationship with you. Now you must do the same with another. In essence, you must bless someone else with salvation, as another has blessed you.

Why do you want to bless another person? Because blessing others is an ultimate Christian value. You bless others because you love them. Some bless others because of natural love, such as a parent to a child. And some bless others because of their friendship, taking them to church where they hear the gospel. Still others bless out of a deep conviction that it is God's will for them to serve others.

Unfortunately, some people bless others for selfish reasons, too. A teacher might do extra things for her students just because she wants the reputation of being a good teacher. Sometimes children may bless their parents because they don't want to embarrass the family. Still others bless for monetary purposes. A server in a restaurant may bless her customers with good service because she wants a good tip.

But true, Bible-motivated blessing is the opposite of selfishness. It never uses others or blesses them to get ahead in life; that's manipulation. You must believe in, love, value and want the best for the other person in order to give them a godly blessing.

I learned a lesson from my good friend John Maxwell. For over 15 years we played golf, always trying to beat the other. As a matter of fact, we kept score over the years, accumulating a record

> You can't go through life trying to defeat everyone and at the same time bless them.

of who had won the most games. Then one day John quit keeping score. He said, "Friends don't keep score." John explained to me that he wanted to add value to my life as we fellowshipped together on the golf course.

I was embarrassed! But from that experience I learned the true nature of how to bless other people. You can't go through life trying to defeat everyone, and at the same time bless them. As a matter of fact, as you grow older, your greatest joy will not be counting your victories but, rather, helping other people win victories. Remember that when you help a friend to victory, you have blessed him or her.

Before You Can Bless Others

- You must add value to them before they will value you.
- You must do something for them before they will do something for you.
- You must draw them to you as you bless them.

So what does it take to bless another person? First, you must be "Jesus" to them because it is really the Lord who blesses other people. This assumes that you allow the Lord to flow through your life, that you exude Christian graces and that you have a testimony that others want to follow. Paul wrote to the Corinthians:

> Now thanks be to God who always leads us in triumph in Christ, and through us diffuses the fragrance of His knowledge in every place. For we are to God the fragrance of Christ among those who are being saved and among those who are perishing (2 Cor. 2:14-15).

Just as a woman's perfume makes others appreciate her loveliness and beauty, you must portray Christ in a winsome way. When a woman enters a conversation with you, her fragrance may add value to your life because you become more aware of God's beauty in the world. In the same way, when you give off the "fragrance" of Jesus Christ, you add the value of enjoyment to others around you.

PRINCIPLE 2: YOU BLESS OTHERS WHEN YOU INITIATE FAITH IN THEM

Remember that there are natural blessings and supernatural blessings. When you do something for others, you may add value to their life in a natural way; a blessing doesn't always have to be spiritually motivated, nor does it need a spiritual objective.

For example, when your neighbor is gone on vacation, you may be asked to pick up the mail and newspaper each day. You help your neighbor in that way, but not necessarily spiritually.

However, suppose your neighbors' parent died. You take food to relieve them of kitchen tasks so they can go about arranging the funeral. You visit in the funeral home and share a word about Jesus Christ. Right there by the casket you pray with your neighbors that God would help them get through that moment of grief. As you offer spiritual help, you bless their lives. You add God's value to their spiritual lives by giving them faith to get through the crisis.

Remember the four men who brought the crippled man to Jesus? They couldn't get into the house where Jesus was teaching because of the crowd. So, climbing onto the flat roof of the house, they removed the ceiling tiles and lowered the sick man down into the presence of Jesus. "When Jesus saw their faith, He said to the paralytic, 'Son, your sins are forgiven you'" (Mark 2:5).

Notice that the text doesn't say that Jesus saw the faith of the crippled man but, rather, that He saw *their* faith—the faith of the man's friends. These four men exercised their faith by bringing the crippled man into the presence of Jesus. They blessed their crippled friend so that he could exercise his faith along with them. In the same way, you bless others when you ignite their faith.

What kind of faith did the four men have? Obviously they had faith in Jesus and His ability to heal. But they also must have had faith in themselves—in their ability to bring the crippled man to Jesus. And their faith must have joined the faith of their sick friend who apparently wanted Jesus' love and His healing touch (see "agree-bless" and "faith-bless" in the glossary).

There are people in life waiting for you to believe in them, just like the sick man was waiting for his friends to believe in him. And when you believe in people, you add value to their lives by helping them believe in God. You initiate faith in people when you help them see what they can become.

When parents bring a young baby to the front of the church for "baby dedication," this is sometimes called blessing the child. Some denominations sprinkle the baby in baptism at this time. Both the parents and all the church believe that this baby can become a follower of Jesus Christ. Therefore they bless the baby, showing that they believe in what the baby can become by growing up in a Christian home.

> ## You initiate faith in people when you help them see what they can become.

When you bless others, don't do it because of who they are or what they can do for you. Rather, bless them for what they can become (see "anticipatory-bless" and "dedication-bless" in the glossary).

Think of some needy person in your life. What does that person need? The greatest need may be for you to tell him or her, "Yes, you can!" You express your faith with the attitude of *Yes, you can overcome your problem and live a better life.* Do you know some struggling people who need you to enter their lives with the attitude that you believe in them? You bless others by expressing belief in them.

Furthermore, you don't just bless "spiritual" people, nor do you just bless Christians. You can bless unsaved people. If they have questions about God, you give them confidence by your answers. If they have doubts about God, you give them the strength to believe in God when you believe in them. If they can't find God, you show them the way to Jesus Christ. You bless them by adding God's value to their lives.

How to Know If You Are a Blessor

- You are glad to be able to bless others.
- Adding value to others comes naturally.
- You get energy from blessing others.
- You are empowered by adding value to others.
- You get satisfaction from blessing others.
- You are happier adding value to others.
- You have a successful track record of blessing others.

The world would be a better place if everyone—believers and nonbelievers—would add value to others; but this initiative usually begins with the Christian. Because we are motivated by God, we must do good things for other people—we must add the value of God to their lives. But the greatest value of all is to initiate in them faith in God. When Jesus said, "Have faith in God" (Mark 11:22), He was giving a command that had the possibility of fulfillment. Because everyone can have faith in God, you bless a person when you initiate his or her faith to know God in a real and eternal way.

PRINCIPLE 3: YOU BLESS OTHERS BY MAKING YOURSELF VALUABLE TO THEM

Have you ever wondered who can bless other people? Can unsaved persons become a blessing to other people? The answer is YES!

They can bless others in a natural way, because they can add value to the lives of other people. When one man helps a neighbor get his stalled lawnmower running again, he has added value to his neighbor's ability to cut his grass and make his home beautiful. That's not the same as spiritual blessings, but it makes the life of both men better.

Can a back-slidden Christian become a blessing to other people? The answer is YES! Even a person who is not in fellowship with God can be a natural blessing to other people. God can use him according to his usability, because God can do all things.

But for God to provide the best blessings, He uses the believer who is walking in fellowship with Him. In other words, the better Christian you become, the more you can bless others. Fully dedicated believers become a channel through whom God works.

Whether you realize it or not, if you are a Christian, you have many gifts and know many things. When you share these with other people, you bless their lives. When you help other employees unlock their computers or fill out a form, you add value to their abilities to do work. When you explain to a friend the spiritual significance of a fast to get an answer to prayer or how to overcome a sin, you have blessed that person. You become valuable to people when you are the one who can help. When you became valuable to others, you add value to them (see "insight-bless" in the glossary).

Even in the secular world, people understand supporting relationships. Albert Einstein said, "Try not to become a man of success but rather try to become a man of value."[1] When we become valuable to others, we are then able to help them. When you add value to the lives of others, they will be drawn to you. What person cannot appreciate those who have helped them? And as you help others, they will love you and want to be with you.

On the other hand, people instinctively know the kind of people to whom they're not attracted.

People You Don't Want to Be Around

- Those who belittle you.
- Those who discourage you.
- Those who criticize you.
- Those who don't believe in you.

No one likes to be around critical people who are always negative and condemning. Life is hard enough. We like to be around those who believe in us and encourage us. We make little room in our lives for those who tear us down.

However, we often have to attend business meetings with critics or work on a project with those who dislike us. We may even have to work closely with those who don't believe in us. But when it comes to our free time, we don't gravitate to them. If anything, we usually block them out of our lives, or we just walk away to leave them to their complaining "circle of one."

So, learn two lessons from the critics. First, while you do not like to be around them, remember also that people don't want to be around you if you are mean-spirited, critical or constantly cutting people down. If you are constantly critical, you can't bless others. Why? Because you're not adding value to their life. So, to become a blessing to others, you may need to make radical changes in your attitude.

Second, even critics and complainers want someone to encourage them. Here's where you can bless their lives, even if they don't bless yours. Jesus told us, "Love your enemies, do good to those who hate you, bless those who curse you, and pray for those who spitefully use you" (Luke 6:27-28). Perhaps by blessing complainers, we can change their lives. Remember that deep down they want love and acceptance. "And just as you want men to do to you, you also do to them likewise" (Luke 6:31). Complainers want to get compliments, so give one to them! You add value to their lives and lay the groundwork eventually to change them (see "compliment-bless" in the glossary).

Maybe certain people can't love you because they don't have the strength to love anyone. So, you can bless their lives by giving them love. And in your gift, they receive the strength to return your love and grow in the ability to love others.

People need what Christians can give them. First, you can give them your testimony (see how inspiring the apostle Paul's testimony was in Gal. 2:20). Second, you can give them acceptance and recognition, i.e., you can bless them with your love. Third, you can give them your faith as you share your testimony of how you became a Christian. When they receive your faith, they become strong enough to reach out to God. Finally, you can give them a blessing and add value to their lives.

Five Things Every Person Needs

- A relationship with God.
- Healthy relationships with others.
- A purpose to live for and ultimately to die for.
- An accomplishment in life.
- A relationship with someone he or she can trust.

As you make your life valuable to others, they become stronger, and they in turn become more valuable to God and others. But you must begin; you must take the first "value" step. The problem is that many do not understand that they need others;

specifically, they do not feel the need of a relationship, especially with someone who is a Christian. So what must you be? First, you must be a friend to them, and second, you must be Christian to them.

Do an experiment now. Make a list of all those people to whom you have added value today. List people you have helped and people who needed you. You can even rank your contribution to them by placing a 1 for adding small value, 2 for adding average value, and 3 for adding strong value to their life.

Now, make a list of all the people who have added value to your life today. This is a list of people who have blessed you, and you've become a better person because of them. You might want to rank these people in the same way, 1 to 3. Are you receiving more value from others than you're giving?

If you are receiving more value than you are giving, think of the small child who must receive more in life than he gives. Babies cannot take care of themselves. But as babies grow to be adults and then parents, they reciprocate by giving to their children what they received initially. However, even a baby is not useless in life. The baby gives happiness to those who care for him. *The question is, Have you given happiness to those who have been adding value to your life?*

PRINCIPLE 4: YOU BLESS OTHERS WHEN YOU KNOW AND RELATE TO THEIR NEEDS AND DESIRES

Sometimes you want to bless others, but they don't want your offer. We would like to share the gospel with all our unsaved friends, but many feel we're just "preaching" to them. Some feel the gospel is an intrusion into their lives. They don't feel lost from God, they don't agonize in sin, nor do they want to change their self-centered lifestyles. When you try to bless them with a spiritual blessing, they reject it because they don't see their need for it.

So what must you do? You can't get them interested in your agenda until you become interested in their agendas. So to bless them you need to know and understand better their aims and dreams, desires and needs. Ask yourself, *What do they want?* and *What do they need?*

But discovering their agendas can be difficult. Learning about other people takes time, intention, energy and sometimes money. But our own self-centeredness may also be why we are not putting forth the effort to understand them. Do we fail to learn about other people's agendas because we are too wrapped up in our own?

A good place to begin is to ask them questions, establishing a bond or relationship with them. And when they answer your questions, value their answers. Perhaps you bless them just by listening to them and valuing what they say.

Eventually you want to point them to God, who ultimately adds value to life. But because they reject your "sermon," or even your explanation from the Bible, it is good to share with them what God is doing in your own life. Since friends share experiences, they should listen to you. If Jesus is in your heart, He will automatically come out in your conversations and experiences. When Peter and John were in prison and they were asked why they testified of Jesus Christ, they could only answer, "For we cannot but speak the things which we have seen and heard" (Acts 4:20).

At times other people will cut off anything you say about God, so you must look for *nonverbal* ways to show them how God will add value to their lives. St. Francis of Assisi said, "Preach the gospel everyday; if necessary, use words."[2] You must share God's Word with others, but not just by preaching. When relevant, share Scriptures that apply to their problem, or help them understand an issue through the lens of Scripture. Whether by word or deed, we are to bless others by putting God's name on them (see Num. 6:27).

Everyone is seeking satisfaction, but not everyone knows that only God can give true happiness (see Ps. 1:1-3). Many people have nagging fears, but you must show them that it is the Lord who gives ultimate confidence (see Phil. 1:6). All people realize that one day they must die, but it is up to you to share Jesus, who is life, with them (see John 14:6).

Then bless their lives by praying for God's blessing on them. Be careful that you don't let prayer be a cop-out for not initiating action; rather, add prayer to the things you do to bless their lives.

To Bless Others Is to Relate to Them

- Look to find their agendas in life.
- Ask questions and value their answers.
- Always point them to God, who adds value.
- Tell them how God can add value to their lives.
- Pray for God's blessing on them.
- Put God's Word upon them.
- Point them to the way that God blesses.

PRINCIPLE 5: YOU BLESS OTHERS WHEN YOU HELP THEM FULFILL GOD'S PURPOSE IN THEIR LIVES

It was Campus Crusade's Bill Bright who first put together the Four Spiritual Laws[3] to be a tool for Christians to use in leading an unsaved person to Jesus Christ. In his first law he gave one of the basic principles that many unsaved people do not understand: *God loves you and has a wonderful plan for your life.* It's an important principle of evangelism to tell others that "God so loved the world that He gave His only begotten Son" (John 3:16) and that He also blesses people with a wonderful plan for their lives.

When you bless unsaved persons, you are pointing them to that wonderful plan. Too often we try to win an unsaved person to Christ by "scaring" him with the threat of hell, death or the unknown. The fear of death does convert some, but negative motivations drive many away. There is a stronger motive: *God's love and providential care for our lives.* God loves people and wants to bless them with a wonderful plan for their lives.

When I played golf in South Korea, I discovered that all the caddies were young women, dressed in saddle oxfords, white pleated skirts and an attractive dark blazer. My caddie was chosen for me because she spoke English. She even graduated from a university with an English major. On the first fairway, I began to share my faith with her, only to find out she was a Christian. With enthusiasm, she told of reading about the Four Spiritual Laws. I carefully drank in every word as she explained, "Buddha never loved me, and Buddha doesn't have a plan for my life—but God does." Then she said, "Because I wanted God's wonderful plan for my life, I prayed to receive Christ."

That day on the golf course I continued to share Bible truths with her. Then she said, "My greatest desire in life is to meet Bill Bright and thank him for writing about the Four Spiritual Laws."

I casually remarked, "I had lunch with him last week, and I'll see him again." Suddenly she erupted emotionally as a typical girl in her early 20s might, crying and laughing. With unbelief she blurted out, "You know the great Bill Bright?"

"Yes."

"Tell him you know a Korean girl who has found God's wonderful plan for her life. My greatest desire is to be a missionary to university students with Campus Crusade."

When you bless others, you are pointing them toward the good things God has for them. Remember, when you bless another person, you are doing good things for yourself as well, because you become happy when he or she becomes happy. And isn't happiness one of the blessings of life?

But also remember that when you bless another person, you are fulfilling your spiritual gift—the ability God has given for service. "Every person has his proper gift from God" (1 Cor. 7:7, author's translation). When you use your abilities to bless others, you fulfill God's plan for your life. Then you bring joy to them, to yourself and to God.

> ## Both the blessor and the recipient are following where God is leading.

There's another thing about the blessor and the recipient. Both are following where God is leading. When Jesus said to fishermen on the shore of Galilee, "Follow Me, and I will make you become fishers of men" (Mark 1:17), He was giving a general principle of fellowship with others as we follow Christ. As you follow Christ, you also will bless others, telling them "how God anointed Jesus of Nazareth . . . who went about doing good" (Acts 10:38).

And what about the persons who receive the blessing? When they receive a spiritual blessing, they begin to look to Jesus, respond to Jesus and follow Jesus. When you bless others, you are helping them to fulfill God's purpose and plan in their lives.

Isn't it wonderful to feel God using you? When you help others find happiness, you can vicariously experience their happiness, thus fulfilling your joy. When you bless others, adding value to their lives, you have done God's will, adding to your reward in heaven. By listening to someone's problems or explaining how to grow in Christ, you properly exercise your gifts; thus, you grow in Christ. Furthermore, you cannot give a blessing without receiving a blessing. Jesus reminds us, "Give, and it will be given to you: good measure, pressed down, shaken together, and running over" (Luke 6:38).

Take-Away Values

- I add value to others when I bless them.
- I add value to others when I initiate their faith in God.
- I bless others when I become valuable to them.
- I add value to others by knowing and relating to them.
- I add value to others when I help them fulfill God's purpose for their lives.

THREE-STEP BIBLE STUDY

A. *Read* each Bible passage.

B. Use the *question* that follows each passage to analyze the passage.

C. Write your *answer* in the space provided.

1. Mark 2:5

> When Jesus saw their faith, He said to the paralytic, "Son, your sins are forgiven you."

How had the men bringing the palsied man to Jesus added value to the life of the sick man?

2. Luke 6:27-28

> But I say to you who hear: Love your enemies, do good to those who hate you, bless those who curse you, and pray for those who spitefully use you.

How and why can you add value to an enemy?

3. Acts 16:30-31

> And he brought them out and said, "Sirs, what must I do to be saved?" So they said, "Believe on the Lord Jesus Christ, and you will be saved, you and your household."

How can you help a person find a proper relationship to God?

4. Matthew 22:37-39

> Jesus said to him, "'You shall love the LORD your God with all your heart, with all your soul, and with all your mind.' This is the first and great commandment. And the second is like it: 'You shall love your neighbor as yourself.'"

What is a person's first step to building proper relationships to others?

5. Luke 9:23-24

Then He said to them all, "If anyone desires to come after Me, let him deny himself, and take up his cross daily, and follow Me. For whoever desires to save his life will lose it, but whoever loses his life for My sake will save it."

What purpose in life can all of us live for and die for?

6. Philippians 1:21

For to me, to live is Christ, and to die is gain.

What is the best accomplishment we can realize in life?

7. Psalm 1:1-2

Blessed is the man
Who walks not in the counsel of the ungodly,
Nor stands in the path of sinners,
Nor sits in the seat of the scornful;
But his delight is in the law of the LORD,
And in His law he meditates day and night.

How can we achieve the greatest blessing, or added value, in life?

JOURNALING

Use the following questions to guide your thoughts and writings in your separate journal.

1. What person has added more value to my life than anyone else (except for my parents)? What and how did he or she do it?
2. What person have I added more value to than anyone else (except for family members)? What did I do? How did I do it? What happened to me because I added value to another?
3. Who has become a better believer because I blessed them? How did I do it?
4. What do I need to do to start adding value to my friends, family and strangers? What do I need to stop doing? To learn? To become?

CHAPTER 4

What Happens When You Bless Others?

Not long ago, a nationwide revival broke out in Argentina, partly because evangelism was tied to the blessing of God. In 1980, approximately 1 percent of the population of Argentina was evangelical. Twenty years later, about 15 percent of the nation had come to faith in Jesus Christ and were identified as evangelical. How did it happen? Obviously, there were outward circumstances, such as the nation losing the war with Britain over the Falkland Islands. The nation's economy collapsed, and its great battleship, the Santa Fe, was destroyed with 655 men killed. But spiritual factors were involved, too—movements such as revival, intense intercessory prayer and spiritual warfare.

WHAT HAPPENS WHEN YOU CHANGE THE APPROACH?

Ed Silvoso was one man God used to bring about this dramatic revival. Ed, an Argentine, had been director of evangelistic crusades for Billy Graham and Luis Palau throughout South America. But after organizing huge programs and spending millions of dollars in advertising; after renting bull rings and soccer fields; after bringing in the best musicians and the best speakers; and after saturating cities with evangelism, Ed resigned. He went back to Rosario, which has a population 700,000 and is one of the cities surrounding the nation's capital, Buenos Aires. He organized people in groups of two to walk around every block in the city, praying for every person in the city that they might be saved. This became known as prayer-walking—praying on site, with insight.

With this action a strategic change, a bold new paradigm, was initiated in evangelism. Whereas most evangelists emphasized negative preaching against sin to convict people or to make them feel bad, Ed decided to bless the people with the goodness of God. After all, he knew that the "goodness of God leads you to repentance" (Rom. 2:4).

After groups of intercessors walked around each block, praying for the people, Ed instructed them to take a notepad and go door-to-door saying, "You have seen us walking around your block. We are praying for every person in every house on this block. How may we bless you?" The intercessors were instructed to write down answers people gave to the question, "What do you want God to do for you?" Unknown to Ed and the intercessors, God would supernaturally use these intercessory inquiries and prayers to create a national appetite for God; and the result was spiritual renewal.

Ed then instructed his intercessors to walk around city hall while the city council met. They asked the mayor, "How can we pray for our city? We want God to bless our city." They did the same at police stations, public schools and other public buildings.

Blessing the unsaved was a radical new paradigm for evangelism. Most evangelists are concerned about the sin of the unsaved. But perhaps just preaching against their sin is not enough to bring them to God. We can entice them with the goodness of God. We can show them there is a better way to live—one in which God blesses their lives.

When you bless another person, you are adding value to his or her life. But what do we mean by "adding value to the unsaved"? We could be talking about adding natural value to others' lives, regardless of the level of their spirituality. This is a natural blessing where you make their lives easier or prosperous.

However, as the people of Rosario, Argentina, discovered, the ultimate added value of a blessing is being brought into a Covenant relationship with God. Often the unsaved cannot perceive this dimension of a blessing, but as the ministry of Ed Silvoso shows, it can happen! Sometimes God uses blessings pronounced on others to accomplish His purpose, even when they are not aware they are doing God's will. In fact, several things can happen when you bless someone.

When You Bless Others

- You speak God's presence into their lives.
- You add strength to their lives.
- You help them find opportunities.
- You intensify your commitment to them.

- You receive answers to prayer.
- You multiply their ministry potential.
- You clarify life's mission both for them and for you.
- You magnify the best in those you bless.
- You testify that you belong to a community of believers.

WHAT HAPPENS WHEN YOU BLESS OTHERS?

What blessings can one person give to another? What blessings can you receive as the blessor?

You Speak God's Presence into Their Lives

When you say "God bless you," you are praying for God to be with the recipient in a special way.

The presence of God in a life has a twofold meaning. First, it is "salvation-blessing," which means the person prays to receive Jesus Christ. As John wrote, "But as many as received Him, to them He gave the right to become children of God, to those who believe in His name" (John 1:12). When that happens, the blessed person can identify with Paul who spoke of "Christ in you, the hope of glory" (Col. 1:27).

The second meaning is "presence-blessing," which means that God goes with the recipient to activate in his or her life the blessing that was spoken. Obviously, to get the full benefit of God's presence, the recipient must receive and act on the blessing. The recipient's faith—mixed with the faith of the blessor—will move God to respond (see Mark 11:22-24; Heb. 11:6).

Note the psalmist's prayer for the blessing of God's presence: "God . . . bless us, and cause your face (presence) to shine upon us" (Ps. 67:1, author's translation).

An example of this presence occurs when we eat the bread and drink the cup at the Lord's table. The bread and wine are symbols of God's presence entering your life. "Jesus took bread, blessed and broke it" (Mark 14:22), and that blessing extends to the partakers of the bread. The blessing of Jesus is His presence that goes with those who properly celebrate Communion. As the bread enters your life through eating, so Jesus enters your life through blessing.

When you bless a child, sometimes you pray for God to raise

> ## As the bread enters your life through eating, so Jesus enters your life through blessing.

a "hedge" of spiritual protection about him or her (see Job 1:10). That hedge of protection is not some mystical wall. It is the Lord Himself in the life of the blessed one, "For the Lord God is a sun and shield" (Ps. 84:11; see "protect-bless" in the glossary).

You Add Strength to Their Lives

When you bless others, you help them do what they are otherwise unable to do. Moses lifted his arms in prayer for Israel to overcome its enemy, the Amalakites; as long as he had the strength to keep his arms raised, Israel prevailed in battle. But when Moses lost physical endurance and dropped his arms, the Amalakites prevailed. Moses needed help to keep his arms extended in prayer.

That's where Aaron and Hur came in. These two men helped Moses do what he couldn't do in his own strength. By holding Moses' arms up for him, they were a blessing not only to Moses but also, as the tide of battle turned in favor of God's people, to all of Israel. When you give your own strength to help others do what they cannot do, you become a blessing to many. Strengthen others by

- looking for opportunities to encourage;
- looking for actions to compliment;
- looking for people to motivate;
- looking for relationships to strengthen;
- looking for alienated people to lift up.

Once a mother of three children was hospitalized. She was understandably worried about her children and husband, but she was also very depressed. She felt that God had abandoned her and that He had not heard her prayers for healing. But the more she prayed for healing, the more depressed she became.

Then her Sunday School teacher visited with several messages for the woman. First, the teacher told how the sick woman's husband had taken responsibility for the children like never before and, in the process, had developed a new love for the children. Next, the teacher told how other ladies in the class had organized a schedule to bring meals into her home. Finally, the teacher shared her confidence that the young mother would be healed, but that it would be in God's time and might take three to four months of rest. The teacher explained, "He who calls you is faithful, who also will do it" (1 Thes. 5:24). When the teacher had left the hospital, the young mother's depression was broken because she saw the plan of God in her life. God had used the Sunday School teacher's hospital visit to bless the young mother.

You Help Them Find Opportunities

One morning I was having breakfast at a restaurant with Bill Greig, chairman of the board at Gospel Light/Regal Books.

As we left the restaurant, I noticed a young father with his son, about one year old. God put it upon my heart to say a few words to the father. I identified myself as a minister and asked if I could pray for his young son. Then putting my hand upon the boy's head, I prayed for him that he would be raised in a Christian home, that he would know the Lord and that God would protect this young boy from the influence of the evil one. Bill Greig identified himself and told of the Presbyterian church he attended nearby.

About a year later, Bill told me that the young father had brought his son to Sunday School at that church. When I laid my hand upon the young boy's head to bless him, I was praying for the boy to have an opportunity to know the Lord and to be protected by God. God answered my prayer by motivating the father to get his son into the house of God.

When the young minister Timothy was facing the pastorate in the city of Ephesus, a task he probably considered too great for him, Paul challenged him, "Stir up the gift of God which is in you" (2 Tim. 1:6). Timothy was to be a pastor of a church that was first pastored by the apostle Paul and then by the apostle John. It's understandable that he didn't feel that he measured up to his predecessors' abilities.

Notice how Paul blessed Timothy. First, Paul pointed out Timothy's strength and his gifts; second, Paul encouraged Timothy to do the ministry that had been given him; and third, Paul reminded him what God could do through him. Paul blessed Timothy by identifying his opportunities to serve the Lord and grow spiritually.

You Intensify Your Commitment to Them
When people think that they have to go through life alone, coming alongside to walk with them is an important way you can bless their lives. In doing so, you may encourage them not to give

up, to keep their spirits up or to do more for God (see "fellowship-bless" in the glossary).

When a boy thinks that his grandfather doesn't even know he's alive, what will it take to change the young boy's life? Perhaps the grandfather adds value to the boy's life by calling him aside to tell him, "You're going to make a great business-man like your father." Next, the grandfather tells him, "I have a trust fund to help you through college." Those words of encour-agement can motivate the young boy to become the business-man that his father and grandfather became. When he's assured that there's a path to make it—there's money to go through col-lege—that's a blessing that can change his life.

In Scripture, when Ruth returned from Moab to Bethlehem, she was a foreigner. She was different from the local people in dress, dialect and many other ways. To use a modern phrase, she stuck out like a sore thumb. But Ruth didn't have to make it alone in a foreign culture. Her mother-in-law, Naomi, supported Ruth, helping her get ahead in her new city.

Naomi told Ruth where she could get a job, then encouraged her to do it, saying, "Go, my daughter" (Ruth 2:2). Naomi knew all the people in the area, so she directed Ruth to the field of a close relative to gather grain for food. Later, Naomi found out that Boaz, a close relative, had a romantic interest in Ruth. The mother-in-law encouraged Ruth to be aggressive: "It is good . . . that you go" (Ruth 2:22). Naomi was a blessing in the following ways:

- Naomi supported Ruth's decisions.
- Naomi encouraged Ruth's faithfulness.
- Naomi shared her wisdom.

Because Naomi blessed her daughter-in-law, they got food, Ruth found a husband, their child was in the line of King David, and Ruth was in the genealogy of Jesus Christ (see Matt. 1:5).

Intensifying your commitment to someone you bless also helps you, the blessor, purify your motives. When you bless another person, you do not do it for your own selfish agenda. Rather, you are focusing on the other person and what is best for him or her. Many people are bound up in their own little, limited world. They have difficulty seeing the needs of others or how they can help another person. When you begin to bless other people, you cannot help but see their problems and identify with them.

> It's amazing what you can
> do in life, if you don't care who
> gets the credit.

There's an old saying, You can't be a Christian alone, which means you cannot live to yourself or for yourself. Because we've been commanded to "love one another" (John 13:34) and to "serve one another" (Gal. 5:13), you will ultimately bless yourself when you first bless others.

In intensifying your commitment to those you bless, you solidify your relationship to them. But it's impossible to bless someone that you hate or envy. When a husband is always criticizing his wife, it's difficult to bless her; nor can a wife bless her husband when she is constantly nagging him.

When there is a "break" between you and a brother or a sister, it's impossible to bless them. Everyone knows that brothers and sisters fight. When you're tempted to destroy your sibling by words, deeds or any other way, you cannot bless them. Have you recently been a blessing to your brothers or sisters? Remember that blessing them is only the first step towards strengthening your relationship to them.

Friendships are not built on sarcasm, but on trust and respect. Do you want your friends to love you? Try blessing them. When you add value to their lives, you solidify your relationship with them.

Many basketball coaches will tell you that they win games because their teams worked so well together. Someone has said, "The main ingredient to become a star is depending on the rest of the team." When any star tries to make it on his own, he destroys the teamwork and the possibility of victory. There's a popular saying in basketball, It takes 10 hands to put the ball through the hoop. Just as in sports, you need others and they need you; the same applies to prayer.

One person cannot make a team successful, but one person can be a crucial ingredient to help make everyone around him a better person. And just as you cannot make others' lives successful (only they can be responsible for that), you can be the key to blessing them. Adding value to them is the first step to motivating them to success. To make this point another way, it can be stated in the negative: Who rejects your blessing?

- Those not in fellowship with you.
- Those not in fellowship with God.
- Those not in fellowship with other believers.

When you bless others by prayer or in any other way, you solidify your relationship with them. As a matter of fact, the deeper you analyze the psychology of blessing other people, the more you come to the genius of Christianity. Blessing another makes you a better Christian.

You Receive Answers to Prayer

One of the key ingredients to answered prayer is the relationship between you and another person. "If two of you agree on earth concerning anything that they ask, it will be done for them by My Father in heaven" (Matt. 18:19). People must learn that praying in harmony with another results in the answer to many prayers that we can't get answered alone (see "fellowship-bless" in the glossary).

What if your prayers are not being answered? Perhaps there is a sin in your heart against another person. You must repair that relationship in order for God to answer your prayers. Remember that Jesus said,

> Therefore if you bring your gift to the altar, and there remember that your brother has something against you, leave your gift there before the altar, and go your way. First be reconciled to your brother, and then come and offer your gift (Matt. 5:23-24).

But sometimes you may not know about a sin you've committed against a brother, or you may be unaware of a sin he has committed against you. Yet, to get your prayers answered, you may need to agree with that person in prayer. So how does this begin?

First, try blessing him. Begin with a natural blessing; anyone can do that by doing something for the other person. Next, give him a spiritual blessing, which moves into the realm of God and the other person's relationship to Him. By blessing the person spiritually, you put yourself on praying ground.

You Multiply Their Ministry Potential

Most of us want to do the best job possible serving the Lord. But look beyond your own ability and beyond your own sphere of ministry. Think what a person you bless can do in serving God.

When you bless that person spiritually, you add spiritual value to their service for God.

Think back to when Saul of Tarsus was first converted. Because he had persecuted the church, not many Christians were willing to trust him. "When Saul had come to Jerusalem, he tried to join the disciples; but they were all afraid of him. . . . But Barnabas took him and brought him to the apostles" (Acts 9:26-27). Probably some thought that Barnabas was foolhardy because he took a chance on a former Christ-hater.

But Barnabas was fulfilling his spiritual gift. He was called the Son of Encouragement (see Acts 4:36), which meant he was a mercy-shower and an exhorter—Barnabas was a blessor. Barnabas did what was only natural; he showed mercy to Paul by introducing him to the Christians in Jerusalem. This was Barnabas's way of blessing Paul. What was the result of this action?

- Paul gained access to the Church.
- He was encouraged for future ministry.
- He and Barnabas became a team for missionary work.

Actually, Barnabas blessed Paul's life at least twice. Almost 10 years later, when Barnabas was planting a church in Antioch of Syria, he needed a strong Bible teacher. He remembered Paul's teaching gifts and that they worked together in Jerusalem: "Then Barnabas departed for Tarsus to seek Saul. And when he had found him, he brought him to Antioch. So it was that for a whole year they assembled with the church and taught a great many people" (Acts 11:25-26).

You, like Barnabas, can increase the potential of ministry by blessing other people.

You Clarify Life's Mission for Both Them and You
When you bless others, you are telling them that you want to be a

"channel of blessing" by identifying with them. You put yourself on God's side and enlist in His service.

But there's a second thing you do. When you bless another person, you are asking him to join with you to serve the Lord together. Just like a young boy tries to get his friend to join the Boy Scouts so they can experience camping together, when you bless another, both of you are joining the service of the King.

You will recall that because Moses sinned against God, he could not enter the Promised Land. But Moses was not bitter, and he became a blessing to Joshua, the soldier who took his place. God told Moses, "Joshua . . . shall go in [the Promised Land]. Encourage him, for he shall cause Israel to inherit it" (Deut. 1:38).

Think of the great accomplishments of Moses. He not only freed Israel from Egypt, but led them for 40 years in the wilderness. Because Moses had talked to God face-to-face and was a friend of God, he had an incredible reputation among God's people. When Moses encouraged Joshua to lead the people into the Promised Land, this was his way of blessing the next leader. Moses not only blessed Joshua, but also he clarified his tasks, assured him of God's anointing and encouraged him to obey the Lord. Joshua became a better leader because Moses blessed him with encouragement and counsel.

You Magnify the Best in Those You Bless

Remember that blessing others is not something you do on your own; you are simply releasing the blessings of God into their life. In Paul's first letter to the Christians in the city of Corinth, he severely criticized them for their sin and was extremely harsh in his condemnation of those who were rejecting the will of God. But in his second letter, Paul wrote to encourage the Corinthian Christians with the blessing of God: "Blessed be . . . the God of all encouragement, who encourages us in our trouble, so that we can encourage other people in trouble, with the same encouragement we originally got from God" (2 Cor. 1:3-5, author's translation; see "support-bless" in the glossary).

We can learn several things from this passage. First, you should bless others with the blessings you get from God. Just as you can't be a blessing by giving your grandchildren an ice-cream cone until you go get it from the soda fountain, you can't bless other people until God has blessed your own life.

Second, when you bless other people, you lift them to the level of your own blessings. Paul lifted the Corinthians to his level by the statement, "Encourage other people . . . with the same encouragement we originally got from God."

The third thing we learn about blessing others from this passage is that it makes us better people. Just as Paul had condemned their sin, now he wants to build them up in the faith.

You Testify That You Belong to a Community of Believers

When you spiritually bless another person, you honestly attempt to obey the words of Jesus, "You shall love your neighbor as yourself" (Matt. 22:39). The foundational basis of your blessing another is the love of God flowing through your heart toward that person.

When you bless another person in the Body of Christ, you are strengthening the Church. Because both of you are members of Christ's Body, your blessing is an aid in carrying out the passion of Jesus:

> Each saved person fits neatly together and is bonded into one Body, so that each person in the Body effectively does what he or she is supposed to do, resulting in the growth in love of every person to one another in the entire Body of Christ (Eph. 4:16, author's translation; see "fellowship-bless" in the glossary).

When you bless another person, it eventually comes back to you through the strengthened Body of Christ. Someone is blessing you while you bless another—and all of you are growing. Both of you have value added to your life and are adding value to others; hence, you are adding value to the whole Body of Christ.

You also testify to the unsaved about the unity of the Body when you bless one another. Remember how Jesus prayed to the Father:

> The glory which You gave Me I have given them, that they may be one just as We are one: I in them, and You in Me; that they may be made perfect in one, and that the world may know that You have sent Me, and have loved them as You have loved Me (John 17:22-23).

As you think about others you can bless—others to whose lives you can add value—you are telling the unsaved that Christians love one another. Just as Jesus did not think of Himself but submitted Himself for the task given to Him, we must not think of ourselves but carry out the work of Christ in blessing other people.

PRACTICAL WAYS TO BLESS OTHERS

Look for opportunities to encourage.
Speak just a word of kindness, support or even appreciation. When you build up other persons, you bless them by adding value to their lives.

You can begin by blessing them with a compliment. That may be the basis for them to bless, or compliment, another person, and from that action they may form a habit, which leads to godly character.

Look for actions to compliment.
When people bless you, you in turn should bless them. When people serve in Sunday School, usher in church or call on the sick, be sure to tell them of your appreciation.

Look for people to motivate.
All of us get tired, for we are mortal. Many people get discouraged, and they need a positive word to keep them going. Other people have stopped serving, and they need your word to start serving again. Everyone needs a kind word while serving the Lord.

Look for a relationship to strengthen.
When you bless the children in your family, you are strengthening both their love for the Lord and their family relationships as well. This bonds the family together. Also, watch for opportunities to encourage children in the church or children wherever you might see them. There are enough people in this world that criticize children or "preach" rules to them. Instead, be one who encourages children, to build them up in the Lord.

Look for alienated people to lift up.
There's always someone who needs a friend; bless him with your friendship. Some people just don't fit in. Remember Barnabas! You can be a Barnabas who brings someone into a Sunday School class. Remember, visitors come to Sunday School on the arm of a friend. You can welcome a new employee at work. Isn't that what Barnabas would do? Since everyone wants a friend, when you bless a person with your relationship you can strengthen that person and move him or her closer to the Lord you love.

TAKE-AWAY VALUES

- I bless others when I make them stronger.
- I bless others by committing myself to them.
- I bless others by showing them opportunities to serve God or grow in grace.
- I purify my motives in life when I bless others.
- I multiply my ministry by blessing others.
- I tell the world I belong to a community of believers when I bless others.

THREE-STEP BIBLE STUDY

A. *Read* each Bible passage.
B. Use the *question* that follows each passage to analyze the passage.
C. Write your *answer* in the space provided.

1. Exodus 17:11-12

And so it was, when Moses held up his hand, that Israel prevailed; and when he let down his hand, Amalek prevailed. But Moses' hands became heavy; so they took a stone and put it under him, and he sat on it. And Aaron and Hur supported his hands, one on one side, and the other on the other side; and his hands were steady until the going down of the sun.

What are the various ways that Aaron and Hur blessed Moses and the Israelite army?

2. Ruth 2:14-16

Now Boaz said to her at mealtime, "Come here, and eat of the bread, and dip your piece of bread in the vinegar." So she sat beside the reapers, and he passed parched grain to her; and she ate and was satisfied, and kept some back. And when she rose up to glean, Boaz commanded his young men, saying, "Let her glean even among the sheaves, and do not reproach her. Also let grain from the bundles fall purposely for her; leave it that she may glean, and do not rebuke her."

In what ways did Boaz bless the life of Ruth?

3. Matthew 18:19

Again I say to you that if two of you agree on earth concerning anything that they ask, it will be done for them by My Father in heaven.

What adjustments do you make to prayers when you bless another by relating properly to them?

4. Matthew 5:23-24

Therefore if you bring your gift to the altar, and there remember that your brother has something against you, leave your gift there before the altar, and go your way. First be reconciled to your brother, and then come and offer your gift.

If you are not getting your prayers answered, what may be one reason? What must you do personally?

5. Acts 9:26-27

And when Saul had come to Jerusalem, he tried to join the disciples; but they were all afraid of him, and did not believe that he was a disciple. But Barnabas took him and brought him to the apostles. And he declared to them how he had seen the Lord on the road, and that He had spoken to him, and how he had preached boldly at Damascus in the name of Jesus.

In what ways was Barnabas a blessing to Paul? How can you do the same thing for someone else?

6. Deuteronomy 1:38

Joshua the son of Nun, who stands before you, he shall go in there. Encourage him, for he shall cause Israel to inherit it.

How did the elderly Moses bless the younger Joshua?

7. Ephesians 4:16

From whom the whole body, joined and knit together by what every joint supplies, according to the effective working by which every part does its share, causes growth of the body for the edifying of itself in love.

What happens to our testimony when we bless other people?

JOURNALING

Use the following questions to guide your thoughts and writings in your separate journal.

1. In what ways have I strengthened the lives of others this past week?
2. Think of some people you know who are about to miss a great opportunity or open door in life. What are they missing? Why are they missing it? How can you bless them by helping them take advantage of this opportunity?
3. Is there someone to whom you'd like to get closer? Why? What could you do to add value to that person's life?
4. Do you know someone who could serve the Lord better? How could you add value to his or her ministry? What should you do?
5. Do you know people who have a poor image of themselves? Why do they have it? How can you bless them to strengthen their self-perception?

HOW TO BLESS CHILDREN

The day was warm and sunny at the church, high on the bluff overlooking the Pacific Ocean. Parents with children in tow arrived at Community Presbyterian Church in Ventura, California, long before the worship service began. A cool ocean breeze created a perfect day for the church's experiment in evangelism.

Flyers had been distributed door-to-door, advertising a special day called Blessing the Children Day, and the attendance was larger than anything they had anticipated. Everyone was invited to "have your children blessed of God." In an age of school shootings, drugs and metal detectors in public schools, parents wanted help; and they came to a local Presbyterian church that offered divine blessings on their children.

This wasn't baby baptism, nor was it baby dedication. The church advertised Blessing the Children as an opportunity to ask divine protection on children—of any age—and a time to pray for children. The church told the community that it wanted children to learn, grow and have a happy childhood. They didn't make it an outward evangelistic event to lead children to Christ, but parents were promised blessings so children would grow in character and faith.

The actual service of Blessing the Children occurred at the end of the morning's sermon. The church elders, along with pastors, were stationed around the inside wall of the church auditorium. Families could choose the leader who would bless their children. Some elders held babies in their arms to bless; some placed their hands on the head of a child in the parent's arms. The larger children stood to receive the blessing as a hand was placed on their head or shoulder.

In some cases, quick counseling was done on the spot as parents told of their children's problems. Others made appointments to get future help. Most elders asked, "How shall I pray for your child?" The church leaders' concern for children opened the hearts of the neighborhood.

In the fall of 1994, I spoke at a minister's convention in West Virginia. The chairman of the denomination's State Board of Christian Education, Reverend Vondie Cook II, was not able to meet me on Friday night for dinner. Rev. Cook's wife was in the hospital; she had just given birth to their son, Chance. I understood and prayed God's blessing on him, his wife and the child.

The next morning Vondie Cook met me at the convention center in Beckley, West Virginia, and got the meeting started. However, he explained that he would have to leave during the morning to pick up his wife and new son. She was to be discharged from the hospital less than 24 hours after their son was born.

We had a wonderful morning convention. After lunch, I had just started my message when, looking down the aisle into the foyer, I saw Vondie and a woman I assumed to be his wife. He was proud as a peacock, holding a bundle that I knew was his newborn baby. I yelled, "Come on in, let's have a look at that baby!"

As Pastor Cook walked to the front, the audience broke into applause, and I announced, "We're going to dedicate this baby to God." I invited the grandmother and grandfather (he is also a minister) to come forward with them for the dedication. Then taking the baby with two hands, I held the child high to God and prayed,

God, our Lord, we offer Chance to You and dedicate him to be Your servant. He has a wonderful father and grandfather, who have served You in ministry. Lord, we pray that Chance would serve You with the same amount of dedication, whether in full-time ministry or wherever You call him.

I dedicate Chance to You, that he would come to trust in You early and understand his salvation and walk in the fullness of Jesus Christ. I dedicate Chance to a life of holiness and service.

Lord, I pray that You would keep Chance from the evil one who would destroy his life. Help him to grow and to learn many lessons; fill him with wisdom and knowledge. Help him understand the spiritual world. May Chance grow up in the Church and may he love the preaching of Your Word in the local church.

Bless Pastor Vondie, his father, that he would raise his son in Your nurture and admonition. Make him a good father. We dedicate Vondie and Teresa to you today for this great task to raise this new baby for Your glory.

We dedicate Reverend and Mrs. Cook to You as grandparents. May they be great examples, wise in counsel, and may they be used in the life of Chance to accomplish Your purpose.

Not everyone who says "God bless you" to a child in fact adds value to the little one. Instead, God has a pattern for you to follow when blessing a child. You should follow that pattern to get His results.

Don't be disturbed that God has a path that you must follow to bless children. There are a lot of things in life that demand the right words. Take my laptop computer. I must use the correct passwords to get into my computer. Only my administrative assistant and I know that phrase, and when we type in the right words, the world of the Internet opens up to us.

You must have the right key to get into the door, the right number to reach someone on your cell phone, the right code to reach your voice mail, the right remote control signal to open your garage door and the right address to get a letter delivered. Then why should we be amazed to find out that God wants us to use His words when we bless another person?

So if you've tried to bless a child and it seems that nothing happens, look for God's pattern, and follow it!

Perhaps the best five steps to bless children are provided by Gary Smalley and John Trent:

Five Steps to Blessing a Child

- Step 1: A meaningful touch.
- Step 2: A spoken word.
- Step 3: Attaching high value to the one being blessed.
- Step 4: Picturing a special future for the one being blessed.
- Step 5: An active commitment to fulfilling the blessing.[1]

When you follow these five steps you may have more success in blessing others. Why? Because God wants to bless people, and He wants to use His people to bless others, especially the children. So when you follow God's steps, you can add value to others' lives as you bless them.

STEP 1: A MEANINGFUL TOUCH

It can pose a catch-22 when I suggest that you touch the person you're blessing. Why? In the case of an adult, some people may misunderstand your intentions when you touch a member of the opposite sex. Even in the case of children, in these days of prolific litigation, some people may think that touching a child involves child abuse. We must simply be aware of the importance of being careful when we touch anyone.

At my church, during baby dedication for Bradford Elmer Towns, my grandson and namesake, I placed my hand on his head as the pastor prayed. My grandson would have none of that. He constantly tried to push my hand away or wriggle his head out from underneath my hand. He was much too young to understand the intent of the blessing. Others around me understood what was happening, and they chuckled because they thought he was cute.

Convey the Blessing with an Embrace

Biblical counselors have given several illustrations of young people who were stunted emotionally because they grew up without the loving embrace of a parent. Some have emotional difficulty simply because they did not experience the acceptance of their parents through a loving embrace. That's because an embrace signifies belongingness.

An embrace says, "You're special." Every child growing up needs to feel special in the eyes of his or her parents. Remember the time you fell down and ran to your mother for an embrace. Suddenly, your world looked better. A mother's embrace adds value to a life, which is another way of describing a blessing.

Sometimes an embrace is a natural blessing. Your daughter completes her piano recital, and as she skips up to you afterwards, you give her a hug. It makes no difference if she did well or not. You embrace her because she's yours and she needs affirmation.

On other occasions, an embrace conveys a spiritual blessing. Perhaps you've just prayed with a little girl, and then you gave her a big hug. Perhaps a little boy has made a decision for God or has correctly recited a Bible verse. Your hug is a spiritual affirmation. You've told these children that you accept them as they seek to serve the Lord.

Convey the Blessing with a Kiss

When Isaac wanted to bless his son, he said, "Come near now and kiss me, my son" (Gen. 27:26). A father conveys love to his son with a kiss. There is perhaps no greater emotional expression to your children than the kiss.

Convey the Blessing by Holding

It's a special time when a grandfather picks up his grandchild and places him on his knee. The grandfather blesses this child by telling him all the great things that he will do on this earth or for God. Sitting on a lap, the child will receive a deeper message than if he only hears it with his ears. To be held on grandpa's lap identifies the child with the past ages, because he is reaching beyond his own natural father.

I remember my grandpa Robert Eli McFadden, Jr., hoisting me up onto his red mule when I was three or four years old. We galloped across a plowed field, racing the mail deliveryman to the rural mailbox, laughing all the way. What a great experience for a grandson and grandfather! Later that night he put me onto his knee in front of the open fire in his bedroom and sang, "De Camptown ladies sing dis song, Doo-dah! Doo-dah!" So what do I remember about my grandfather? That I liked him and he liked me. I remember feeling special.

Even Jesus held the children as He blessed them. "And [Jesus] took them up in His arms, put His hands on them, and blessed them" (Mark 10:16). What better example to convey blessing upon children than to do it as Jesus did.

Convey the Blessing by Touching the Head

Quite often when I bless a baby, I place my hand on its head and pray God's blessing upon the child. Recently Connie Nylander, a former secretary in the religion department here at Liberty University, brought her daughter, McKenna Grace, to the office. She reminded me that I had blessed little McKenna Grace when she was first born and then again when she was 10 months old. Now a toddler, I picked her up and, placing my hand on her head, blessed her again.

Why did I do that? Because I believe God answers prayer and will bless little McKenna's life with added value simply because I prayed blessings upon her. I also prayed that God would keep her from the evil one. Protection is an essential part of the blessing. Then I prayed that when she comes of age, McKenna would accept Christ.

One of the reasons I know God will bless this child in answer to prayer is because her mother, Connie, is a godly young woman who also prays for McKenna. The Lord promised that "If two of you agree on earth concerning anything that they ask, it will be done for them by My Father in heaven" (Matt. 18:19). Connie and I joined together to ask God's blessing on McKenna.

In the Scriptures we have the illustration of Jacob placing his hands on the heads of his two grandsons as he blessed them.

"[Jacob] stretched out his right hand and laid it on Ephraim's head . . . and his left hand on Manasseh's head" (Gen. 48:14). We know that blessing with a touch was an act of faith, because the writer of Hebrews indicated, "By faith Jacob, when he was dying, blessed each of the sons of Joseph" (Heb. 11:21).

Other Ways to Bless with a Meaningful Touch
You tell people that they are valuable with a handshake or when you reach out to hold hands as you "pray-bless" them (see glossary). Holding hands may be a way to add value to their lives. You're telling them that they are special just by touching them.

In Bible times, people seemed to be more demonstrative than we are today. They hugged, kissed, embraced and held one another. In a day when it's politically incorrect to touch a child, your actions and desires must be above suspicion. When you do it, make sure you have the approval of parents, or other supervising adults. There are Bible illustrations of meaningfully touching a child in love and acceptance to build up the child's ego and self-perception.

STEP 2: A SPOKEN WORD

God has chosen to use the spoken word to bless a person. Those who hear you speak the Word of God into their lives receive added value—a natural blessing because they know you affirm them—and they receive a spiritual blessing because of the power of the Word. Also, the spoken word adds the power of faith when you speak (see Mark 11:23). Some might suggest you don't need to speak a blessing, saying that you can privately pray or bless a person and God will respond by adding value to the recipient's life. Certainly your private intercession will touch the life of the person you blessed. The Bible, however, emphasizes *speaking* the blessing.

God instructed the priests how to bless Israel, "*Say* to them: 'The LORD bless you and keep you'" (Num. 6:23-24, emphasis added). Notice what God said the blessing included. "[The priests] shall put My name on the children of Israel, and I will bless them" (Num. 6:27). The priests must speak the blessing they want on the people and verbally say the name of the Lord upon them.

The Importance of Speaking the Blessing

First, verbalizing a blessing is important because what's in a person's heart comes out of the mouth (see Matt. 15:18)—or, as the old farmer said, "What's in the well comes up in the bucket." Words are important to God because they reveal the intent of the heart. In conversion, God wants a convert to say with his mouth, "Jesus is Lord." So when you speak a blessing, what you really want God to do for the child comes out of the depths of your heart.

Second, when you speak a blessing over a person, he or she hears what you have said. You put God, as well as your faith, on the spot. A spoken blessing may be a seed of faith. "If you have faith as a mustard seed, you will say to this mountain, 'Move from here to there,' and it will move" (Matt. 17:20). Therefore, don't just think a blessing silently nor pray a blessing inwardly. Speak the blessing over the child because your words activate your faith and the faith of others.

A third thing happens when you speak and he or she hears the blessing. The two of you have "agreed together." God uses agreement because it is outward, expectant and honoring to God. "If two of you agree on earth concerning anything that they ask, it will be done for them by My Father in heaven" (Matt. 18:19). When you pray a blessing in agreement with another, you will receive the blessing.

We have noticed that it was "by faith Isaac blessed Jacob" (Heb. 11:20). But notice how this was a *spoken* faith. Remember,

Isaac was living in tents in the desert. He had not gained title to the land he wanted to give his son. He only had meager resources for an inheritance. But Isaac had faith that God would keep His promise to him and to Abraham by multiplying Jacob's seed physically and spiritually—and it was important for him to verbalize that faith.

So in the blessing Isaac said to Jacob, "You shall not take a wife from the daughters of Canaan" (Gen. 28:1). Isaac plainly said that the blessing involved a condition that Isaac was to be separated from the sinful tribes surrounding them.

Then, Isaac was told, "Take yourself a wife from there of the daughters of Laban your mother's brother" (Gen. 28:2). To receive the blessing of God there was a marriage condition that Jacob had to understand clearly. The blessing was tied to holiness; he had to be separated unto God.

There was another verbalized aspect of Isaac's blessing to Jacob. "May God Almighty bless you, and make you fruitful and multiply you, that you may be an assembly of peoples" (Gen. 28:3). Here the blessing is a prediction that his son would grow into a mighty nation. When Isaac spoke this blessing, there were probably only two or three dozen people in the camp. The father spoke the blessing of prosperity upon his son by faith, but it was not just faith kept in his heart; it was faith spoken so that all could hear.

So when you bless, speak outwardly for both you and the recipient to hear. Especially when you bless children, not only should they hear what you say, but also the parents, grandparents and those who influence the children should hear what you foresee (see "predict-bless" in the glossary).

The Influence of the Tongue in Blessing
God continually reminds us that our tongue controls our lives. The Bible describes the tongue as being like a bit in a horse's

mouth that guides the powerful animal where it shall go. The tongue is also like a small rudder on a mighty ship, turning it about (see Jas. 3:3-4). So our tongue directs our life. And James added that "no man can tame the tongue. It is an unruly evil, full of deadly poison. With it we bless our God and Father, and with it we curse men, who have been made in the similitude of God" (Jas. 3:8-9). You can bless children with your tongue, or you can hurt them. The wrong use of the tongue is surely involved when our blessing doesn't seem effective. Here are some reasons why your blessing doesn't work:

- You haven't been blessed.
- You don't bless in faith.
- You don't follow God's pattern.
- You bless the wrong thing.
- You bless the wrong way.
- You bless the wrong person.

Because our words are our life, when we bless with our mouth, we pledge our life to the one we bless. When a baby is brought before a church in dedication, the parents pledge to raise that baby in the "nurture and admonition of the Lord." The pastor pledges the church's support to raise that child, and all "agree together," asking God to bless the child. But the congregation members go further. With each pledge, they promise to work together to bring about God's blessing upon the child.

Counselors Smalley and Trent give several illustrations of how our words influence our children. By constant criticism we tear down their self-esteem and make them feel insignificant or of little value. But when we praise our children, we add value to their lives. When you pray for children, you raise their level of expectation and you add your support that you think they can overcome challenges.

As a small boy, my mother took me to her family graveyard near Sardinia, South Carolina, where there stands a large, 10-foot granite stone that lists the original members of her family, the McFaddens, who settled the area in 1732. The stone listed each generation from John McFadden to the present. The McFadden

---

Because our words are our life, when we bless with our mouth, we pledge our life to the one we bless.

---

stone was a symbol of family pride and stability. My mother said to me, "Remember who you are; make me proud of you. You can do anything you put your mind to do." She was setting the bar of expectations high. As I stood before that massive stone, I felt the heavy obligation of my forefathers upon my young shoulders. The stone was a challenge for me to do what they did. Now, I've not been able to do all I wanted to do, but that doesn't mean I didn't try. My mother did not call it a blessing when she stood me in front of that stone, but she did pass on to me family expectations. It had the same impact of a blessing.

Your words can tear down your children's self-esteem and emotionally handcuff them for the future. When you tell your daughter, "Your room is always dirty," you make her seem less valued in your eyes and hers. When you tell your son, "You're not as smart as your sister," or "You're so clumsy," what have you said to him? You've told the child that he is a loser. If you criticize children enough, eventually their self-perception will say, *I'm a loser*.

My friend John Maxwell says that we put symbolic numbers on children's foreheads by the way we react to them. When you tear down a child by saying, "You're so clumsy," it's like putting a low number—a 1 or a 2—upon his forehead. You've made him feel about as low as possible.

On the other hand, when you praise a child for an outstanding term paper or when his team wins a Little League game, you're putting a 9 or a 10 upon his forehead. Your compliments build strong self-esteem. When you speak a blessing, you help children see themselves through God's eyes.

I don't like illustrations from poker, but there's some truth in the fact that sometimes we make life a kind of card game. Every time you tell a child he is dirty, dumb or a failure, it's as though you are dealing that child a "loser card." And when a child spends his life gathering loser cards, what happens when he gets ready to get into life's game? If all the child holds is loser cards, usually the child "folds." To be a winner in poker, you've got to have "winner cards." And what are winner cards? When you say to a child, "That's wonderful," "You're great," "That looks cute on you," "Congratulations," those are winner cards. Why don't we deal such cards more often? Here are some reasons we don't praise others:

- We feel it will take away their motivation.
- We feel it inflates their ego.
- We feel uncomfortable doing it.
- We don't mean it.
- We think they know it without our saying it.
- Our parents didn't praise us.
- We think they will take advantage of us.

You can give many excuses for not praise-blessing the young. But whatever reason you give, it doesn't have any weight compared to the lost opportunities. When you use words of praise or blessing, you build them up, you prepare them for the future, and you make them solid believers.

STEP 3: ATTACHING HIGH VALUE TO THE ONE BEING BLESSED

When you bless others, you are giving them high importance in your sight; and when you speak God's name over them, you're giving them importance in God's sight.

If you love your children, they will know it. When you bless them with words, they'll feel it. Remember that the word "bless" in Hebrew means "to kneel." When you bow to a king, you are indicating his importance in your life. So when you bless others, you are saying that they are important to you. What do you do by putting a 10 on their forehead? You are making them important in your eyes, and you enhance a special relationship between them and God.

After a terrible storm, a father ran through cut glass and twisted corrugated roofing, looking for his son. Finally he found him. Later, as his feet were being bandaged, the father was asked, "Didn't you feel the lacerations on your feet?" He answered, "No, I was holding my boy." How precious are your children to you?

Jacob blessed his son Judah saying, "Judah is a lion's whelp" (Gen. 49:9). What did he mean by that? The same thing we mean today when we think of a hard-driving young businessman as a young lion. The same thing we think of when a new, extremely aggressive football player has a will to win. When you call someone a young lion, you are predicting a certain type of success in life. A young lion will achieve great things by strength and aggression.

When Jacob blessed another son Issachar, he said "Issachar is a strong donkey" (Gen. 49:14). What did he mean in saying this about his son? Since a donkey is a burden bearer, a worker and the one that can be counted on, Jacob was saying that Issachar as a faithful son would carry well the burdens of responsibility. Others could count on him because Issachar himself would bear their burdens.

We like to have people like Issachar around because they solve our problems, they make life easier for us and they are a blessing to all. Some may blush at calling a son a donkey, but if you examine this carefully, calling Issachar a donkey was a blessing that predicted his future. As Issachar grew older, he tried to live up to his father's expectations by being faithful, helping others and adding value to everyone around him.

When Jacob blessed his son Naphtali, he said he was "a deer let loose" (Gen. 49:21). What was he saying about the future of this son? Jacob was saying that Naphtali was beautiful because everyone appreciates the grace and form of a young deer, whether running through the field or drinking silently at a stream. Jacob was saying to his son, "You do things right; other people admire you; you are artistic, appropriate and picturesque." When Jacob pointed out this potential in his son, Naphtali tried to fulfill that prediction. Hence, the blessing given by his father became a reality in life.

Shortly after his baptism, Jesus was introduced to Simon Peter. When he first met the husky fisherman, He said, "You are Simon the son of Jonah" (John 1:42). The Greek word "Simon" comes from the Hebrew word "Simeon," which means "listener." Peter's parents named him Simeon when he was born. But if anything, Peter never listened to anyone. Peter was blunt, strong and self-reliant. But a *listener*? No! So when Jesus met Simeon, He gave the big fisherman a new name: "'You shall be called Cephas' (which is translated, A Stone)" (John 1:42).

Simon was now known as Rock. And when you think of a rock, what comes to your mind? Something that's dependable, solid and firm? While giving him a new name was not technically a blessing, it was a prediction of what Peter was to become.

On several occasions Peter still showed his weakness by being blunt and crude. The Master had to rebuke Peter for telling Him not to go to Jerusalem, where he planned to die (see Matt. 16:21-23). On another occasion, Jesus rebuked Peter because of his boastful attitude, claiming he would never deny the Lord (see Matt. 26:34-35). Peter bragged like an immovable rock, but when he failed, he was hardly a rock. However, when the Lord needed a solid man to introduce the Church on the Day of Pentecost before a large and hostile crowd of Jews, Jesus chose Peter to be the spokesman. Why? Because Peter was a rock. He had become the name Jesus gave him.

STEP 4: PICTURING A SPECIAL FUTURE FOR THE ONE BEING BLESSED

When you bless someone, you are not dealing with the past and probably not the present. You are pointing them to the future. When Isaac blessed Jacob, he pointed out how God would use him in the future. Isaac blessed Jacob, saying, "Let peoples serve you, and nations bow down to you. Be master over your brethren, and let your mother's sons bow down to you" (Gen. 27:29). God had chosen Jacob to be the father of the 12 tribes of Israel. So when Isaac blessed Jacob, he was predicting that he would be over his brothers and the family would bow to him. What a special future!

John Maxwell gave his granddaughter a special name, Sunshine. In giving her this name, he was telling everyone that his granddaughter brought special joy to his life. Don't you think that granddaughter will always try to bring sunshine into the life of her grandfather?

When you bless a child, try to make it open-ended. Just as water cannot rise above its source, children usually do not arise above the expectations we put upon them. When you say to a child, "You'll never be much of a teacher," you may be limiting that child's future. While some use negative motivation to try to bring out the best in a child, be careful that you don't put so much baggage on the child that you kill his or her initiative. It is possible to allow too much sun to burn a flower or to water a plant so much that you drown it. In the same way, it is possible to give too many compliments to your child or to be too critical of them. Isn't balance the key to life?

Make your blessings and expectations consistent with both your past actions and theirs. When a young boy shows promise in sports, praise him by challenging him to be a winner. When a young girl shows excellence in caring for others, point out her mercy, perhaps challenging her to be a nurse.

Don't be so foolish as to bless a child toward a goal that is unreachable or unmanageable. For the young man in braces with polio, don't challenge him to become a track star. And for the young child who has little ability in science or schoolwork, don't challenge him to be a doctor. Be realistic! Since blessing is adding value to children's life, challenge them to the next *attainable* goal in their life.

STEP 5: AN ACTIVE COMMITMENT TO FULFILLING THE BLESSING

When you bless someone, you are making a commitment to that person. This means you shouldn't walk through the mall trying to lay your hand in blessing on every person you see. Why? Because you must carry out the blessing you give.

When you bless others, it should be because you have a relationship with them. Through that relationship, you are focused to help them reach the blessing you speak. If you can't do something for or with the person you bless, at least you can pray for him or her.

When I walk through my Sunday School class before it begins, saying "God bless you," or "Blessing on you," is that an empty pattern? I hope not, for I have committed myself to helping class members by teaching them the Word of God. I have prayed for them to live the biblical principles I teach. So when I say "God bless you," I know I've made a commitment to helping them receive the blessing that I speak.

Do Something Involved With the Blessing

When you bless a child (or anyone else), you have an obligation to help accomplish what you have spoken. When a grandfather blesses his grandchildren to receive education or to "be the best you can be," what should that grandfather do? He should take time to teach his grandchildren, or pass along values to them, or put money into an account to help them get the education they need to reach their goals in life.

Just to walk by someone and say "God bless you" without following up with your good works does not fit into God's pattern. "If a brother or sister be naked, or destitute . . . and you say to them, 'God bless you,' but you do not give them anything, what good is that?" (Jas. 2:15-16, author's translation). Your blessing is empty when you pray God's blessing on a person but do nothing to help fulfill your blessing.

Share What God Has Given You

Again, consider Jacob. His father had said to him, "May God give you of the dew of heaven" (Gen. 27:28). That was symbolic of the prosperity God would put upon the things Jacob's hand would touch. Many years later when Jacob came to the blessing of his grandsons he said, "God, before whom my fathers Abraham and

Isaac walked, the God who has fed me all my life long to this day . . . bless the lads" (Gen. 48:15-16). Just as a shepherd lives outdoors, experiencing the dew of heaven to grow the grass that his sheep eat, Jacob was blessing his grandchildren with God's provision for them.

Involve Their Best Interest

You bless children not for your own good, but to add value to their lives. Sometimes in ministry it can be self-deceptive to bless people. If you don't "mind your motives," you may want them to be blessed so you will have a more successful class or church. Will God honor that motive? No! You bless people for their best interest.

As Jacob was blessing his grandchildren, notice how the blessing was described. "He blessed them, *every one with the blessing appropriate to him*" (Gen. 49:28, *NASB*). This means that when Jacob blessed his 12 sons, each one received a different blessing that was appropriate to his strength, his passion and his future.

What does this mean for you? It means you must be wise, knowing the person that you are blessing. You must be insightful, understanding what the child, if he or she is old enough, desires for the future and how he or she plans to live for God. And you must have deep faith that God can give the blessing for which you pray. Since everyone has an appropriate blessing, learn what is appropriate to each person before you attempt to bless him or her.

Become a Student of Those You Intend to Bless

Before you bless others, you must know something about them. Otherwise, how can you make the blessing appropriate to them? Your blessing might be empty words. Have we not heard someone pray, "Lord, bless him"? What we often do *not* hear is what the blessing is or how the person might help accomplish a blessing. To speak a specific blessing, you must know the person, which means you must become a student of those you intend to bless.

What must you know? You must know a little bit about their nature and how they solve their problems. You must understand their dreams, the things they want to do in life. What about their potential? What are they good at? And where is their passion? And don't forget their spiritual gifts. In the case of older children, in what areas has God given them ability to serve Him? All of these combine to make the character that determines what they want to do in life. Then when you know them, your blessing can give direction and meaning to their lives.

Become a Teacher to Those You Intend to Bless

You want to bless others by pouring your life into them. Therefore, you must become a teacher to those you bless. "Train up a child in the way he should go, and when he is old he will not depart from it" (Prov. 22:6).

When a father speaks a blessing upon his son, commending him for his good play in a Little League baseball game, what else must the father do? Obviously, if he wants his son to be a winning sportsman, the father must take him to games, practice with him, build him up after defeats and praise him after victories. If you want your son to be a winner, you must pour a winning attitude into him. Socrates said, "Why do ye . . . take so little care of your children, to whom one day you must relinquish it all?"[2]

Take-Away Values

- I can protect children from danger by blessing them.
- I can add physical and spiritual value to children by blessing them.
- I can reinforce blessings by a meaningful touch.
- I must speak the blessing over them audibly.
- I must value them as individuals before I bless them.
- I attach a special future by blessing them.
- I must become active in fulfilling the blessing I speak.

THREE-STEP BIBLE STUDY

A. *Read* each Bible passage.
B. Use the *question* that follows each passage to analyze the passage.
C. Write your *answer* in the space provided.

1. Genesis 48:14

> Then Israel stretched out his right hand and laid it on Ephraim's head, who was the younger, and his left hand on Manasseh's head, guiding his hands knowingly, for Manasseh was the firstborn.

What do you think when you see someone place a hand on the head of a child to bless them?

2. Numbers 6:23,26

> Speak to Aaron and his sons, saying, "This is the way you shall bless the children of Israel. Say to them: . . . The LORD lift up His countenance upon you, and give you peace."

Why is speaking important when blessing a child?

3. Mark 10:16

And He took them up in His arms, laid His hands on them, and blessed them.

What special message is communicated to children when you hold them to bless them?

4. Matthew 15:18; James 3:8-9

But those things which proceed out of the mouth come from the heart, and they defile a man.

But no man can tame the tongue. It is an unruly evil, full of deadly poison. With it we bless our God and Father, and with it we curse men, who have been made in the similitude of God.

Why does God put emphasis on our words?

5. Genesis 49:28

> All these are the twelve tribes of Israel, and this is what their father spoke to them. And he blessed them; he blessed each one according to his own blessing.

We should not exaggerate or claim unreachable things when we bless children. What should direct the content of our blessing for a child?

6. Proverbs 22:6

> Train up a child in the way he should go, and when he is old he will not depart from it.

Since you must know the child to give them an appropriate blessing, what also must you do?

7. James 2:15-16

> If a brother or sister is naked and destitute of daily food, and one of you says to them, "Depart in peace, be warmed and filled," but you do not give them the things which are needed for the body, what does it profit?

A spoken blessing may not be enough. What else must we do when blessing someone?

JOURNALING

Use the following questions to guide your thoughts and writings in your separate journal.

1. How will you bless your children? Will you place your hands on their heads, their shoulders, or will you hold them?
2. Why are your children valuable to you? How are they valuable to you?
3. What things can you do today to add value to their lives? Make a list.
4. How do you feel about the pattern suggested in this chapter for blessing your children? What aspects of the pattern will you use?

CHAPTER 6

You Can Receive the Blessings of Abraham

Perhaps the best-known scriptural references about blessings are God's promises to bless Abraham, as found in various forms in the book of Genesis.

Abraham lived among heathens. He knew very little about God until the Lord called him to leave his home country and family. God asked him to go to a place he didn't know (see Gen. 12:1). It was a place very different from where Abraham lived. Because Abraham believed and obeyed God, the Lord promised to bless him in seven different ways. This sevenfold blessing is central to the entire sweep of the Bible—God's calling out the Jews as a people of His own and the extension of this blessing to "the new Israel," the followers of Christ. It also provides an important background for the blessings believers speak upon others today.

The seven blessings appear the first time God spoke to Abraham (when he was still known as Abram).

The Sevenfold Blessing to Abraham

1. I will make you a great nation;
2. I will bless you
3. And make your name great;
4. And you shall be a blessing.
5. I will bless those who bless you,
6. And I will curse him who curses you;
7. And in you all the families of the earth shall be blessed (see Genesis 12:2-3).

This passage is well known because it became the basis for God's care and direction of the Jewish nation. And in the promise that through Abraham "all the families of the earth shall be blessed," the blessing even contains the promise of the coming Messiah, i.e., Jesus Christ. The apostle Paul would later write:

> What's more, the Scriptures looked forward to this time when God would accept the Gentiles, too, on the basis of their faith. God promised this good news to Abraham long ago when he said, "All nations will be blessed through you." And so it is: All who put their faith in Christ share the same blessing Abraham received because of his faith (Gal. 3:8-9, *NLT*).

Since we live by faith, as Abraham did, cannot we claim the blessings given to Abraham? While there is only one *interpretation* to every passage, and the interpretation here applies first to the nation Israel, there are many *applications*. This passage can be applied to our life today in several ways.

1. Natural and Spiritual Family Blessings

God first promised Abraham, "I will make of you a great nation" (Gen. 12:2). This is God's promise to make Abraham a large and prosperous nation. The Jews are God's people, and He has promised to prosper them. Satan knows this and has tried to eliminate the Jews on many occasions. Yet, while Israel today is small among the nations of the earth, substantial numbers of Jews live in many nations around the world. God has blessed the Jewish people, and He is beginning to fulfill His promises to Israel.

In the same way, if you are a believer in Christ with the faith of Abraham you can claim the physical and spiritual blessings of God upon you and your family. What does this mean? That God can add value to your children, that they can be influential, and that you and your family can be greatly used of God.

You can pray, *Lord, use me and my family to extend Your kingdom on Earth.*

2. Financial Blessings

In the second part of God's promise to Abraham, He said, "I will bless you" (Gen. 12:2). In spite of persecution and the Holocaust, wherever you find the Jewish people they tend to rise, like cream, to the top. Whether it's their tenacity, their indomitable spirit or the influence of their heritage, Jews often seem to prosper. Is not this God's blessing upon them?

What can you do as one person with the faith of Abraham, who also believes in the Messiah? You can claim the financial blessings of God.

The financial blessing of God is not "the prosperity gospel." God has not promised that you will be superrich or that you will win the lottery; your financial ship will not come sailing into the harbor. To misinterpret the Scriptures in this way is to create false financial expectations. Into some lives, even among the faithful, God promises persecution, trouble and, in some cases, even martyrdom. Some who are quick to look for verses that seem to promise financial prosperity never seem to see the verses that promise temptations, trials and persecution.

Since blessing means added value, don't live your life looking for the $100 million jackpot in the state lottery. Rather, be happy when you get a 3 percent raise, because that adds a little value to your checkbook. Learn to be equally happy with God's small blessings and large blessings. And if you suffer financial reverses, rejoice when God gives you spiritual blessings.

Pray, *Lord, give me this day my daily bread.*

3. The Blessing of Influence and Testimony

God promised Abraham, "I will make your name great" (Gen. 12:2). God has fulfilled this promise. The name Abraham is one of the most recognized names among the religions of the world. At least three religions know his name well: he is the father of faith to Christians, well known as a prophet in Islam and revered among the Jewish people as the first Hebrew.

How does this apply to you? Ask God to bless your testimony so that others are spiritually blessed through you and your godly reputation.

Pray, *Lord, bless my influence so that my life and service will add value to Your kingdom.*

4. The Blessing of Effective Service

God promised Abraham, "You shall be a blessing" (Gen. 12:2). Through Abraham God has spoken to the world. Through the children of Abraham have come the Scriptures that are the foundation of both Judaism and Christendom. The Old Testament prophets were Abraham's offspring who spoke and wrote the Word of God. Old Covenant priests who ministered to God and kings who ruled for God were from Abraham. Without this foundation, there would be no New Testament. Our rich foundation of the Old Testament gives credibility to God's promises to us in the New Testament.

How can this promised blessing bless your life? Just as God used Abraham in His service, ask God to bless your service for Him. Whether you are an usher in church, sing in the choir, work behind the scenes making telephone calls and mailing letters or testify to others, ask God to bless your service for Him. Just as God promised to bless Abraham, He can bless you.

Lord, bless my service for You.

5. The Blessing of Healthy Relationships

God promised Abraham, "I will bless them that bless you" (Gen. 12:3). Notice how God has kept His Word. The nations that have honored and protected Israel have been blessed of God. Because the United States of America has opened its arms to the Jewish people, as well as those of every other race, God has blessed the United States.

The Jewish people in turn have blessed America with financial prosperity, scientific advances, literary greatness and artistic excellence. Just as the United States has received and protected those Jews who were persecuted elsewhere, America has been used in our time to care for the underprivileged of the world. One of the reasons God has blessed America is evidenced in our nation's care of the Jewish people.

Ask God to make you a blessing to every life you touch. When people honor and respect you, be sure to give honor to God for His blessings.

Lord, help me add value to the lives of others in every way possible.

6. The Blessing of Protection

God promised Abraham, "I will curse him who curses you" (Gen. 12:3). This is God's promise to punish those who persecute the children of Abraham. Whether that person is Nebuchadnezzar, Josef Stalin or Adolph Hitler, I believe they all failed in their overall goals because they persecuted the Jewish people. Currently in the news, Israel is vilified and attacked by Saddam Hussein, Osama bin Laden and Yasser Arafat. Because God has promised to curse those who curse Israel, these leaders and others who hate Israel will not prosper.

What does God's blessing of protection to Abraham mean to you? First, pray that God will protect you from those who hate you. Inasmuch as the blessing is applied within a spiritual context, this relates to those who persecute you for your spiritual testimony.

And what should be your response to those who persecute you? Jesus told us, "Bless those who curse you, and pray for those who spitefully use you" (Luke 6:28). One of the best ways to handle critics or antagonists is to pray God's blessing upon them. That means you have dealt with your emotions, and you want to add value to their lives, even though they are attempting to harm you.

When you pray for your enemy's salvation, you reflect your honesty and faith. Paul told us, "If your enemy is hungry, feed him; if he is thirsty, give him a drink" (Rom. 12:20). By blessing our enemies with good deeds, we witness God's love to them. Notice the second half of that verse. When your enemy turns his back on God, yet you do good to him, "In so doing you will heap coals of fire on his head" (Rom. 12:20)—a sign of shame that might lead your enemy to turn to God because of your blessing.

Lord, give me the ability to bless those who persecute me.

7. The Blessing of Salvation

God promised Abraham, "In you all the families of the earth will be blessed" (Gen. 12:3). This is a reference to the coming Messiah, Jesus Christ, who made salvation available to all: "the Lamb of God who takes away the sin of the world" (John 1:29). Jesus is "the way, the truth, and the life. No one comes to the Father but through Jesus Christ" (John 14:6, author's translation).

When you share Jesus Christ with a lost person, you bless others with the greatest blessing of all. And how do you share? Sometimes you become a prayer intercessor, blessing unsaved persons through your prayer. At other times, you bless them by sharing your testimony. As you tell them how you came to know Jesus Christ, you motivate them to salvation. Your life can become a testimony to others, just as the lame man stood to demonstrate God's healing power: "And seeing the man who had been healed standing with them, they could say nothing against it" (Acts 4:14).

At other times, you must go beyond just sharing your testimony with them. You must present the plan of salvation and motivate them to be saved. "Knowing, therefore, the terror of the Lord, we persuade men" (2 Cor. 5:11).

Lord, use me to win others to Jesus Christ.

TO RECEIVE BLESSINGS, YOU MUST GIVE THEM

Humility is the very essence of Christianity, "If anyone desires to come after Me, let him deny himself" (Luke 9:23). Too often we think only of what's good for me—what will help my reputation, what I enjoy eating or what makes me happy. But you cannot fulfill the Christian life just being inwardly focused. You must be outwardly motivated. You can go through life being a blessing to others if you continually ask, "Lord, how can I add value to other people?"

THREE-STEP BIBLE STUDY

A. *Read* each Bible passage.
B. Use the *question* that follows each passage to analyze the passage.
C. Write your *answer* in the space provided.

1. Genesis 12:1-2

> Now the LORD had said to Abram:
> "Get out of your country,
> From your family
> And from your father's house,
> To a land that I will show you.
> I will make you a great nation;
> I will bless you
> And make your name great;
> And you shall be a blessing."

What "internal event" had to occur in Abraham's heart in order for him to obey this command, and why might this have been difficult? (Hint: see Hebrews 11:8.)

2. Genesis 15:2-3

> But Abram said, "Lord GOD, what will You give me, seeing I go childless, and the heir of my house is Eliezer of Damascus?" Then Abram said, "Look, You have given me no offspring; indeed one born in my house is my heir!"

What problem did Abraham face in believing God's promise that he would become the father of many nations?

3. Genesis 17:7-9

> "And I will establish My covenant between Me and you and your descendants after you in their generations, for an everlasting covenant, to be God to you and your descendants after you. Also I give to you and your descendants after you the land in which you are a stranger, all the land of Canaan, as an everlasting possession; and I will be their God." And God said to Abraham: "As for you, you shall keep My covenant, you and your descendants after you throughout their generations."

What did God require of Abraham and his descendants in response to God's promised blessings?

4. Genesis 17:20-21; 18:10-15

And as for Ishmael, I have heard you. Behold, I have blessed him, and will make him fruitful, and will multiply him exceedingly. He shall beget twelve princes, and I will make him a great nation. But My covenant I will establish with Isaac, whom Sarah shall bear to you at this set time next year.

And He said, "I will certainly return to you according to the time of life, and behold, Sarah your wife shall have a son." (Sarah was listening in the tent door which was behind him.) Now Abraham and Sarah were old, well advanced in age; and Sarah had passed the age of childbearing. Therefore Sarah laughed within herself, saying, "After I have grown old, shall I have pleasure, my lord being old also?" And the LORD said to Abraham, "Why did Sarah laugh, saying, 'Shall I surely bear a child, since I am old?' Is anything too hard for the LORD? At the appointed time I will return to you, according to the time of life, and Sarah shall have a son." But Sarah denied it, saying, "I did not laugh," for she was afraid. And He said, "No, but you did laugh!" (Gen. 18:10-15).

Who would be "the son of the promise," and why did Abraham's wife, Sarah, laugh at God's promise that she would bear this child?

5. Acts 3:12,25-26

So when Peter saw it, he responded to the people: "Men of Israel, why do you marvel at this? Or why look so intently at us, as though by our own power or godliness we had made this man walk? You are sons of the prophets, and of the covenant which God made with our fathers, saying to Abraham, 'And in your seed all the families of the earth shall be blessed.' To you first, God, having raised up His Servant Jesus, sent Him to bless you, in turning away every one of you from your iniquities."

How do believers in Jesus know that they are heirs to God's promise to Abraham?

JOURNALING

Use the following questions to guide your thoughts and writings in your separate journal.

1. What evidence does the author cite for God having richly blessed the descendants of Abraham? Can you think of additional evidence that God is faithful to His covenant with Israel?

2. What are your thoughts about the financial aspect of God's promise to bless His people? Do you sometimes have doubts about this? After writing down specific questions you may have or have heard others express, write a prayer asking God to strengthen your confidence that He will keep this part of His Covenant with you.

3. How do you think God has enabled you to be a good influence? Write a prayer asking Him to extend your spiritual influence on specific people in your life.

4. Obviously, faithful believers suffer and eventually die. How can this be in keeping with God's covenant blessing with Abraham, and thus with believers today?

APPENDIX

BLESSING AT THE BIRTH OF A CHILD

(fill in the name of child)

Of all the blessings I can give you,
May you know Christ and have eternal life.

Of all the blessings that will guide your life,
May you be blameless in character and live for Christ.

Of all the wealth with which I can bless you,
May you have a spirit to work hard, a spirit of excellence in
diligence and a spirit of happiness in each job well done.
Of all the protection I can bless upon you,
May you receive God's will and live under the protection
He gives.

Of all the marriage blessings I can give,
May you marry well, may you fulfill your life in your family
and may God's love be reflected in your love for your mate.

Blessing on a New Marriage

_________________________ and _________________________
(fill in couple's first names)

May you have the love of John the apostle,
The patience of Job,
The wisdom of Solomon,
And happiness enjoying one another.

May you work hard as Rachel and Jacob,
Live as long as Elizabeth and Zechariah,
Service others as Aquila and Priscilla,
And prosper spiritually in Christ.

May you make good decisions as Esther,
Understand the future as Deborah,
Put God first as Ruth,
And grow in Christ together.

May you have answers to your prayers,
Solutions to your problems,
Enough money to pay your bills,
And good health to enjoy life.

Finally, may you pursue God's heart as David,
Be effective in service as Paul,
Be meek as Moses,
And have as many children as Israel.

DAILY PERSONAL REMINDER
(A BLESSING FROM PSALM 1)

Blessed is the man
>Who walks not in the counsel of the ungodly,
>Nor stands in the path of sinners,
>Nor sits in the seat of the scornful;

But his delight is in the law of the LORD,
>And in His law he meditates day and night.

He shall be like a tree
>Planted by the rivers of water,
>That brings forth its fruit in its season,
>Whose leaf also shall not wither;
>And whatever he does shall prosper (Psalm 1:1-3).

GLOSSARY

agree-bless **23, 51**

When the blessor and recipient agree in prayer for the blessing they ask (see Matt. 18:19).

anticipatory-bless **52, 70**

When you bless someone based on the embryonic potential you see in them (see Gen. 1:28; Mark 11:22-24; Luke 6:38; John 15:11).

appropriate-bless **9, 34, 70**

When the recipient of a blessing both receives and acts on the blessing given to him (see Gen. 39:5).

ask-bless **12, 14**

See **pray-bless** (see Lev. 6:23-26; Deut. 28:3,5,12).

benediction-bless **31**

Invoking God's blessing on a church audience as it leaves a service and the special presence of God; "speaking" God's presence to go with each person (see Lev. 6:23-26; 2 Cor. 13:14).

Bible-bless   **35**
When the blessor speaks the Word of God over the recipient (see Rev. 1:3).

blessing-expectation   **25, 69, 91-93, 100, 103, 104, 117**
Being careful that a blessing flows out of the person's past actions and potential in life (see Gen. 49:28; Mal. 3:10; Rom. 2:4).

blessor   **9, 32, 36, 53, 79-80**
The person in fellowship with God who blesses the life of a recipient (see Acts 4:36-37).

communion-bless   **37, 72**
See **fellowship-bless** (see Ruth 2:4; Mark 14:22).

compliment-bless   **56, 79, 80, 101**
When you give a compliment to a person so that God uses you to bless the recipient with stronger self-esteem (see Luke 6:31; 2 Cor. 1:3-5).

dedication-bless   **23-24, 52, 89-91**
When you ask God's natural and supernatural prosperity on a venture, event, thing or equipment (see Mark 10:16).

evangelistic-bless   **39, 58**
When the blessor shows the recipient the plan of salvation or prays over the recipient so that he or she will come to salvation (see Luke 6:28; Acts 4:20).

faith-bless   **34, 51**
Trusting God to give the blessing for which you pray and experiencing the inner confidence of His working (see Matt. 17:20; Heb. 11:20).

fellowship-bless 75, 78, 81

When your relationship to a person is tied to the blessing you speak for him or her (see Eph. 4:16).

harmony-bless 78

See **fellowship-bless** (see Matt 18:19).

insight-bless 54

When the blessor asks God to give the recipient spiritual understanding.

intercede-bless 34, 89-91

When the blessor prays in behalf of the spiritual needs of the recipient as a blessing is given (see Heb. 11:21; c.f. Gen. 27:26-29).

natural-bless 9, 15-16, 22, 37, 60-61, 116

When you add value to the normal life of a recipient, without necessarily appealing for supernatural intervention (see Gen. 39:5; Job 1:10; Matt. 5:45).

praise-bless 34, 50, 89-102

Using words of praise to build others up (see 2 Cor. 2:14-15).

pray-bless 17, 90, 91, 96

To ask God for His blessings on a person (see Lev. 6:23-26).

predict-bless 52, 70, 98

To speak an outward blessing about what you want to happen in a person (see Luke 24:50-51).

presence-bless 9, 17, 51, 71, 105-108

When the recipient receives in faith a blessing for God to be with them to carry out the blessing (see Ps. 67:1; Mark 2:5).

prosper-bless   9, 37, 73, 98, 116

When the blessor speaks God's promise of physical and material blessing into the recipient's life (see Gen. 28:3; Deut. 28:1-4).

protect-bless   8, 9, 37, 72, 119

When you pray for God Himself to become a hedge around the recipient's life to protect him or her from the evil one (see Gen. 12:3; Ps. 84:11; 128:5-6; Rom. 12:20; Heb. 13:6).

recipient   9, 15

Used in connection with blessings, a recipient is the person who is receiving a blessing (see Gen. 30:27).

salvation-bless   69-71, 120

When the recipient prays to receive Jesus Christ for personal salvation (see Gen. 12:3; Mark 10:14-16; Luke 6:28).

speak-bless   9, 17, 34, 96-97

When the blessor says aloud the blessing over the recipient, knowing by faith that God will do what is said. *See also* **faith-bless** (see Num. 6:27).

spiritual-bless   9, 16-17, 28, 116

When your blessing causes a person to know God or grow in Christ (see Eph. 1:3).

support-bless   59, 72, 81, 83

When the blessor speaks God's blessing to demonstrate his or her support for the recipient (see Prov. 8:21; 2 Cor. 1:3-5).

table-blessing   11, 29, 35

Thanking God for the food at mealtime and asking that He

would use the food to prosper the physical body (see Mark 6:41).

warfare-bless   29, 85

When the blessor intercedes to God against spiritual oppression (from Satan or demons) for blessings on the recipient (see Gen. 14:19-20; Exod. 17:11-12).

worship-bless   12, 30, 78

When the focus of blessing on a recipient is to worship or magnify God (see Ps. 103:1; Matt. 5:23-24; Jas. 3:8-9).

ENDNOTES

Introduction

1. Gary Smalley and John Trent, *The Gift of the Blessing* (Nashville, TN: Thomas Nelson, 1993).

2. Jack Hayford, *Blessing Your Children* (Ventura, CA: Regal Books, 2002).

Chapter 2

1. See my book *Praying the Lord's Prayer* (Ventura, CA: Regal Books, 1997).

Chapter 3

1. *The New Encyclopedia of Christian Quotations*, s.v. "success."

2. *The New Encyclopedia of Christian Quotations*, s.v. "witness."

3. Bill Bright, *Have You Heard of the Four Spiritual Laws?* (Orlando, FL: New Life Publications, 1965).

Chapter 5

1. Gary Smalley and John Trent, *The Gift of Blessing* (Nashville, TN: Thomas Nelson, 1993), p. 19.

2. *The New Encyclopedia of Christian Quotations*, s.v. "children."

Also from Elmer Towns

Fasting for Financial Breakthrough
A Guide to Uncovering God's
Perfect Plan for Your Finances
Elmer L. Towns
Paperback • ISBN 08307.29631

Fasting for Spiritual Breakthrough
A Guide to Nine Biblical Fasts
Elmer L. Towns
Paperback • ISBN 08307.18397
Study Guide • ISBN 08307.18478

Prayer Partners
How to Increase the Power
and Joy of Your Prayer Life
by Praying with Others
Elmer L. Towns
Paperback
ISBN 08307.29348

Praying the Lord's Prayer for Spiritual Breakthrough
Daily Praying the Lord's Prayer
as a Pathway Into His Presence
Elmer L. Towns
Paperback • ISBN 08307.20421
Video Study Package
UPC 607135.002901

Praying the 23rd Psalm
"The Lord is my Shepherd;
I shall not want"
Elmer L. Towns
Paperback • ISBN 08307.27760

What Every Sunday School Teacher Should Know
24 Secrets that Can Help
You Change Lives
Elmer L. Towns
Mass • ISBN 08307.28740
Video • UPC 607135.006091

Available at your local Christian bookstore.
www.regalbooks.com

Experience the Blessings That Surround Us All

Blessing Your Children
How You Can Love
the Kids in Your Life
Jack W. Hayford
Gift Hardcover
ISBN 08307.30796

Blessed Are the Peacemakers
Finding Peace with God,
Yourself and Others
Neil T. Anderson
and *Charles Mylander*
Paperback • ISBN 08307.28910

Experience the Blessing
Testimonies from Toronto
John Arnott,
General Editor
Paperback
ISBN 08307.27663

The Secret Place of Joy
Finding God's Place of Joy for
You—and Living There Every Day!
Lindell Cooley
Paperback • ISBN 08307.27957

Simple Prayers for a Powerful Life
How to Take Authority Over Your
Mind, Home, Business and
Country
Ted Haggard
Paperback • ISBN 08307.30559

Discover Your Spiritual Gifts
A Self-Guided Quiz
Includes Explanations
of All Spiritual Gifts
C. Peter Wagner
Paperback
ISBN 08307.29550

God's Word for Your World™

Available at your local Christian bookstore.
www.regalbooks.com